Moses Beech

Ian Strachan

Moses Beech

Oxford University Press

Oxford   New York   Toronto   Melbourne

Oxford University Press, Walton Street, Oxford OX2 6DP

Oxford London Glasgow
New York Toronto Melbourne Auckland
Kuala Lumpur Singapore Hong Kong Tokyo
Delhi Bombay Calcutta Madras Karachi
Nairobi Dar es Salaam Cape Town

and associated companies in
Beirut Berlin Ibadan Mexico City Nicosia

Oxford is a trade mark of Oxford University Press

British Library Cataloguing in Publication Data

Strachan, Ian
  Moses Beech.
  I. Title
  823'.914[J] PZ7.S892/ 80-41297
  ISBN 0-19-271451-1

Photoset in Great Britain by
Rowland Phototypesetting Limited
Bury St Edmunds, Suffolk
and printed by Biddles Limited
Guildford, Surrey

Chapter 1

ALTHOUGH it was only half-past three the snow, which had been falling all day, made it unusually dark. What had been a light, gentle fall in the morning had by now turned into a full scale blizzard but I was still determined to make it to Manchester.

The hood of my anorak was pulled down almost to my eyebrows and my body bent against the wind so that snow slid off on to the legs of my jeans leaving cold, dark patches which grew larger during the afternoon. My brown, canvas baseball shoes were squelching up water like a sponge and my socks, acting like wicks, drew it further up my legs. Every now and then I had to stop and scrape off the treacherous platform of ice which repeatedly built up on the soles of my shoes, making every step I took a lottery.

I heard the steady drone of a car, picking its way along the ill-defined road, coming up from behind me, and stuck out a wet, blue thumb to attract the driver's attention. The note of the engine did not change and I turned to glare at the driver. His car was almost a travelling snow-drift. The windscreen wipers just managed to clear portholes for him to peer through and the heat from the headlights left the car with snowy eyebrows. I don't think he even saw my outstretched hand. The car swept past sending a black arc of sludge over the hedgebank and me.

His car left black tracks on the road but fresh snow soon fell in those. At first it melted into brown but soon the soft, obliterating snow regained its hold and very quickly all sign of his existence had gone.

As I trudged on, my face raw as liver from the snow which clung to my eyebrows and eyelashes, I grew to hate the stuff. On Christmas cards it always looked so soft and fluffy; this was like having handfuls of needles flung at you.

The wind increased steadily during the afternoon causing the snow to drift, making it impossible to tell what was road or verge and I found myself stumbling over hidden tussocks and into disguised grids, cursing myself for ever setting out. I also realised it was soon going to be dark. Being used to the city street lights I didn't realise how early, or quickly, it went dark in the country. I obviously wasn't going to get a lift, or make Manchester, by nightfall, nor was it going to stop snowing and it seemed like a good idea to find somewhere to shelter.

It was some time since I'd seen any kind of house but I wasn't feeling fussy, a barn would do, if I could find one. Anything to get out of the cold, driving snow.

After another agonising hour of slipping and sliding along the road I turned a bend and, through the gloom ahead of me, saw the blue flashing light of a police car. I nipped across the verge and crouched in the shadow to see if I could tell what was going on and how long they'd be likely to be there.

A car must have skidded off the road. It was lying awkwardly, one wheel in the ditch its bonnet up in the air. There were two policemen and someone who must have been the driver. Quite obviously they were not going to be able to get the car back on the road themselves, they must be waiting for a breakdown truck and, on a night like this, that could mean waiting for hours.

With little else to do while they waited, the two coppers were bound to notice me if I shambled past like the abominable snowman. They'd start asking questions, I'd start mumbling, then they'd get suspicious. Next they'd probably get me checked out using their radio, just to see if I was who I said I was, and the next thing I'd be on my way back. I hadn't struggled through the blizzard of the year to end up sitting in the back of a police car, although in one way the prospect of being anywhere warm and dry was tempting.

I retraced my steps, at least I would have done if they hadn't already been filled in with snow, to a turning I'd passed a few moments earlier. I guessed that if I went down there I might be able to get back on to the main road beyond the accident and the eagle-eyed police.

This side road, unlike the main road, probably hadn't been used all day, so the snow was deeper and my progress grew slower and slower. My legs ached with the effort of heaving them out of the snow each time, only to have them sink back in again. Each footstep was costing more effort than it was worth, I told myself, as I stumbled through knee-deep, undulating drifts of snow. And my idea that I would have a chance to get back to the main road disappeared as the road swung away to the left and started to climb a steep hill.

At one point I saw a light ahead of me and thought I might be able to find some shelter, but the road I was on kept turning obstinately away from it and I certainly wasn't prepared to risk cutting across open fields. I was already beginning to have visions of the next day's newspaper headlines:

'DISILLUSIONED BOY DIES IN BLIZZARD.'

By now I was cold, wet, hungry and starting to get frightened. The lights I had seen had long since disappeared into the murk, the drifts were getting deeper and there only seemed to be an individual fruit pie between me and the hereafter.

What little advice I'd ever read about survival trickled round in my head, but most of it seemed to involve climbing into plastic bags, which you just happened to have handy, or to depend on a survival kit that stows away in a fountain pen until you need it. My duffel bag contained a change of clothes, my post-office savings book and some writing paper. I was more prepared for writing my will than surviving.

Hunger must have made me light headed because the next thing I remember, was running, or rather blundering, at high speed across the snow.

If I'd met those policemen then I would willingly have given myself up. Come to think of it, if they'd seen a lunatic charging

7

around in the snow like me, they'd have either leapt into the car and driven off or arrested me on the spot as a public danger.

I had no idea what I was doing or where I was. I just leapt, fell, raced and charged round and round in the banks of snow. I think I was crying; I know I was shouting. Shouting all kinds of things. A few last words, some thoughts on religion which I felt needed saying but fit for nobody's ears but mine, and every four lettered word I could think of, but the howling wind threw them back in my face.

I lashed out at the darkness and the snow as if it might give way under enough pressure. I cursed my luck, my judgement, which had landed me in this mess, and being born.

I crashed in and out of drifts in blind panic. Eventually the inevitable happened, I caught my foot under a tree root and fell full length. This was no fluffy, friendly, Christmas-shop-window snow, but solid like rock and my face smashed right down on it.

I lay there trying to get my breath back and felt pain at both ends of my body. My ankle was at least twisted and possibly broken; my face was sticky with what I knew must be blood from my nose and I wondered if that too was broken. I remember lying there wondering if a broken nose might give me a certain appeal with girls. How I ever expected to see a girl, or anyone else for that matter, ever again, I don't know, but I wasn't being rational any more.

Probably I passed out about then because the next thing I remember was rolling over to look at my ankle, by what little moonlight there was, and realising I couldn't see it. I stretched out a hand and there was nothing there. My hand and ankle didn't connect. I thought about chronic frost-bite but then slowly realised that what I could feel was snow.

However long I'd been lying there the snow had drifted over the lower half of my body and was rapidly advancing up my chest. For a moment a strange kind of hypnotic tiredness overtook me and I nearly lay back with the clear intention of letting the snow finish the job off, but at the last moment I pulled myself together and dragged my body up.

Using a tree trunk to heave myself up, probably the one I'd

fallen over, I wiped as much snow as possible from my face and body, then tried the ankle. Never having broken one before it wasn't easy to tell if I had now, I only knew that it hurt like the devil if I put much weight on it, but that if I was going to survive I had to find some kind of shelter before it gave out altogether.

Again I saw a faint light, maybe it was the same one I'd seen earlier. It seemed perfectly possible I'd been going round in circles. This time I decided to make straight for it even if it turned out to be a mirage.

Every step was agony but after what seemed like hours I'd covered enough ground to realise that it really was a light and then I became determined that I would make it.

When I reached the house the snow had covered the path and a good deal of the hedge so that I couldn't find a way into the garden. There was no sign of a gate. By now the pain in my leg was burning and I decided this was time to throw away convention. I blundered straight through the hedge and made for the lighted window.

After trying to find a gate I hadn't the strength to look for a door, in any case I didn't want to risk passing out before I succeeded, so I hammered on the window and shouted above the howl of the wind, until my throat felt raw. It took my last ounce of energy. I felt myself slipping down the wall and back into the snow but then I thought I heard the squeal of bolts being drawn and the sound of a man's voice.

A light flashed across my face but by then I'd lost interest, it was time for somebody else to take over.

Chapter 2

W HEN I came round I thought at first I was dead. There was this old bloke with white hair, looking like Old Father Time, peering down at me and he was holding a candle.

'Don't try to move,' he muttered.

Straight away I knew I wasn't dead because wherever I was due to end up this wasn't the place for two reasons. One, the man spoke with a strong country accent and two, his remaining teeth were either black or brown and I'm sure heaven and hell will have their quota of dentists.

'Where am I?' The words were out before I could stop myself. It had always sounded a phoney line on the telly and I'd vowed I'd never say it if the opportunity arose. Well, it had and I had.

'Park Cottage,' the old man said, proving what a daft thing it was to ask, for I was none the wiser. 'Has somebody attacked you?'

'No,' I said feeling a real fool, 'I fell over.'

'I'll get you a hot drink,' he said, turning away from me, and everything went dark. I thought for a second I'd passed out again until I realised he'd taken the candle away and the only other light came from an oil lamp on a table in the middle of the room.

The old man was pouring water from a soot-blackened kettle, which rested on a hook above a blazing log fire in an old fashioned blacklead range, into a brown teapot. As he blew into a blue, enamel mug, to remove the dust I suppose, the fire projected a macabre shadow of him across the ceiling.

Just my luck! I run off, get lost in a snowstorm, and end up with some prehistoric caveman.

He shuffled back with the tea, dragging the metal tips of his boots across the red quarry tiles, to where I lay on a big, black horsehair sofa. The trail of black slush from the back door to the sofa made it clear that, as I was unconscious at the time, he must have carried me and that he was a good deal stronger than he looked.

'Drink this. It's hot, mind!'

It was as strong as creosote, tasted as if he'd put at least a pound of sugar in it; I hate tea anyway but it was very welcome. My teeth chattered against the tin mug as I sipped the syrupy liquid. Outside I'd got so cold I'd felt nothing but a kind of numb pain all over. Now that I was starting to thaw out I was shivering from head to foot, but the heat of the tea still wasn't reaching me through the sides of the mug.

'Hurt yourself when you fell?'

'My ankle.'

'Sit still. I'll look.'

He folded back the damp leg of my jeans and removed my soggy shoe and sock with hands that felt like glasspaper. When he touched the ugly brown-green swelling I nearly dropped the mug and hit the ceiling.

'You can't walk on that. Where were you making for?'

'Manchester,' I said it quickly and avoided looking him in the eye. 'I was on my way to see an Uncle of mine.'

'Walking all the way?'

'I was going to hitch a lift but when the weather got bad nobody stopped and then I must have taken a wrong turning.'

'You did that all right. What about your parents? They'll be worried, you being out in this.'

'No, they won't.' I kept sipping the tea and hoping he'd stop asking questions before I'd got my wits about me.

He rubbed his unshaven chin with his scrawny, brown horn of a hand then shambled off to the door. As he pulled it open a cloud of snowflakes went scurrying across the tiles. He slammed it shut and rubbed the back of his head thoughtfully as the lamp and candle recovered from the blast of cold air.

'You can't go out in that. You'll have to stay the night.'

'It's very good of you.'

'There's no choice. You'll have to sleep on that couch though, there's nowhere else.'

'I'll manage.'

'You'll have to. But tomorrow you'd better get a doctor to look at that ankle.'

'I don't need a doctor,' I said, rather too quickly. 'I'll be all right after a bit of rest.'

'I'm not keen on doctors either, but if you're ever going to make it to Manchester it'll need seeing to. I'll get you some water. If you bathe it it might take some of the swelling down. You must be daft as that back door being out dressed like that in this weather.'

'Yes, well . . . .' my excuses trailed out.

'I doubt you'll walk on that ankle tomorrow.'

'I'll have to won't I?'

'You will. You can't stay here. I'll get us a meal.'

He turned abruptly away and went off to peel potatoes in the brownstone sink at the end of the room. He was obviously a man of few words which suited me very well. Once the potatoes were on he attacked a tin of Irish Stew with a fearsome looking can-opener, which looked as if it might have been used for emergency operations on suits of armour during the Civil War.

Although he moved slowly his pace was steady and deliberate. I guessed he must be in his seventies at least. His skin was weather-beaten to a tan like an old leather wallet. Even the top of his head shone like a small, polished table. Clearly he'd spent most of his life out of doors.

His hair was white, thin and straggly. With the fringe around his bald patch, and the clumps of hair escaping from his ears and nostrils, he looked a bit like a toy that's losing it's stuffing.

Although the whites of his eyes were a watery yellow the irises were intensely blue.

A three day grey, black, silver stubble hung over the neck of

12

his striped, flannel union shirt which he wore without a collar. His blue overalls were shapeless and the jacket which he wore over them had shiny patches which reflected the lamplight like the patches of ice I'd seen in the road.

'You still look blue with cold,' he observed, 'come and sit nearer the fire.'

I hopped unsteadily across the room. My jerky movements sent sharp pains through the injured ankle and I was relieved to reach an upright, wooden armchair beside the range.

'You can wash that blood off your face later.'

I felt the scabs of congealed blood around my nose but at least it didn't feel broken any more. As the heat from the fire warmed me steam began to rise from my jeans.

'You should get out of those wet things.'

By the time I'd struggled out of my damp clothes and hung them in a line on the brass rail above the range he'd returned downstairs with some clothes of his. We were about the same height but he was a good deal bulkier and it needed a piece of stout string to take up the slack. Even so, I must have looked like a sack tied in the middle. The clothes smelt of mould and stale tobacco but at least they were thicker than mine and dry.

The room, like his clothes, was more serviceable than comfortable. There was no carpet, just a rug which might have been any colour when new but was now mostly grey with dust. A vast cupboard with a set of drawers beneath filled one wall from floor to ceiling. The only other furniture, apart from a couple of armchairs by the fire, consisted of an old treadle sewing machine with a bakelite radio sitting on it, a huge round wall clock above it, and the main table with its oil lamp in the middle of the room.

'Pull a chair up,' the old man said as he slapped two steaming, piled plates on to it.

The half we sat at had clean newspaper spread on it, like a tablecloth, but the other half held everything you were ever likely to want during a meal, and a few you weren't. Sauces, pickles and jam jars rubbed shoulders with a mousetrap, some fishing line, a trowel, an odd collection of cutlery, a misshapen

13

loaf and some elderly fruit pies with enough mould on them to glow in the dark.

'Find yourself a fork,' he said and settled down to ladling lumps of scalding potato into his mouth with a great slurping sound.

I found a reasonably clean knife and fork and joined him. Potatoes and tinned Irish stew might not sound the greatest meal you've ever tasted but to me, that night, it was terrific. He hacked two slices of bread off the loaf, we mopped up the gravy and sat back, full to the gills.

He hadn't spoken throughout the meal, just kept his eyes on his plate and slurped up the food. When I'd tried to be polite and complimented him on the meal he'd just grunted.

As soon as he finished eating he collected the plates, dumped them in the sink, then flopped down in one of the fireside chairs and indicated I should sit opposite.

Maybe living alone for so long he'd forgotten how to talk unless it was necessary. I watched him pull the charred, stubby remains of a pipe out of his bib pocket together with a small, silver penknife which he used to carefully remove every scrap of dottle from the bowl of his pipe. Once satisfied he replaced it with brown curls of fresh tobacco plucked from a yellow, floppy-rubber pouch which he pressed home with the end of the silver knife.

After a few trial sucks, he lit the pipe with a paper spill from the crowded mantelshelf. The whole performance had an air of ritual about it, but the result was a vile smelling haze of blue smoke which fogged the lamplight and enveloped us both. He could have achieved the same result, with far less effort, by throwing old cabbage leaves on the fire.

He seemed well pleased though, sat back in his chair and, between wheezes and coughs which sounded as if they came from a punctured set of bagpipes, launched into conversation so abruptly that he startled me.

'Where are you from?' he demanded.

'The Potteries.' There seemed no harm in telling him that much.

14

'Never been there.'

'Never?' I didn't like to sound incredulous but if I could get here from there in a day travelling at snail's pace you would have thought he'd have got a bus or something once in his life.

'I don't like cities.'

'Oh,' was about the best I could manage.

'Full of mean people with mean ideas. Have you got any parents?'

'Just two.' I decided to lay on a little sarcasm.

'You surprise me,' he said, exhaling a vast cloud of smoke. 'From what I hear, folks in cities chop and change their marriages around so that you could have anything up to half-a-dozen parents. What do they think about you gadding about like this?'

'They don't bother about me, whatever I do.'

The old man watched me carefully through the cloud of acrid smoke.

'They know I can take care of myself.'

'Take care of yourself?' he looked down at my ankle resting on the tarnished brass of the fender. 'Seems to me you could get lost in your own back yard.' I felt myself blush as I turned away to watch the fire dance. 'When I was your age I had to be in by a certain time or my Dad leathered me. You didn't do anything twice against him. Seems to me you young people take no notice of your elders, you just run everything your own way. I was brought up with a few cuffs round the ear, which did me no harm.'

'Did it do you any good?'

'Well,' he said slowly, 'it stopped me giving cheek to grown-ups.'

'Sorry.'

He didn't ask any more questions of a personal kind after that. We chatted about my journey and he kept asking what the snow was like when I passed so-and-so, or if a particular field was covered. Of course I didn't know half the answers because I didn't recognise the places or the names he used, but he seemed satisfied with what little I could tell him.

15

He probably got few visitors up there and was interested in every detail he could pick up about the outside world, but especially in anything that happened in the five miles around his house. How he managed without a telly I couldn't imagine and the radio looked so old I couldn't believe it still worked.

When he'd gleaned everything he could from me he set off telling me about the old days and the snows he remembered from the past.

It's an odd thing. Whenever old people tell you about the past you begin to feel you've met an American tourist. Everything they tell you about is bigger, hotter, and worse than anything you've ever experienced.

Every now and then he'd lapse into silence just gazing into the fire and puffing at his pipe. At first I found these silences, no matter how short they were, a bit disconcerting. Silence at home was ominous. It was the quiet before the storm. In our house the telly was always on, day and night, and one of the three of us would probably be yelling our head off until the other two joined in, and for a while we drowned the racket of the telly.

Here the silences were friendly. The tick of the clock nodding the time away, while the wind roaring around the door and window made sitting in front of the log fire seem a very cosy occupation. It had much more character than a two-bar electric fire even if it did leave your back feeling the chill.

With the physical exercise I'd had, coming into the warm after the bitter cold outside, and being stuffed with food, I began to feel my head nodding on to my chest. My eyes tried to watch the flickering flames but kept closing.

'Time for bed,' the old man said. He knocked his pipe out on the bars of the range and stuffed it into his bib pocket without a second glance. The clock chimed ten. I'd thought it was much later, which just showed how exhausted I was.

'If you want to wash there's hot water in the kettle and cold in the bucket. I'll get some blankets.'

I'd seen the old man grasp the handle of the kettle and thought I could do the same. He must have had hands like asbestos

16

though because it burnt my hands, even when I tried a second time using the belly of my jersey to carry it to the sink.

When the old man was getting the meal I hadn't realised what a makeshift arrangement the sink was. There were no taps and when you pulled out the plug the water just ran through into a large bucket which was already pretty full and had some evil looking grease floating on it.

As I washed I glanced into the mirror which hung from a rusty nail just above the sink. No wonder the old man thought somebody had attacked me! My face was a complete patchwork of mud and blood which made me look like the survivor of a traffic accident.

The injury to my nose had scabbed over so I washed the rest off only to discover I'd got a ripe, black eye.

'Got everything you need?' the old man asked as he dropped a pillow and some old blankets onto the couch.

'Yes, thanks. It's very kind of you to put me up.'

He tugged open the curtains and let the light spill out. Huge flakes of snow flashed past and disappeared into the hostile darkness.

'I didn't have much choice, did I?' he let the curtain drop back into place. Using his hand as a shield he blew the oil lamp out. 'I'll take the candle, you can see all you need with the light from the fire. If you're thinking of stealing anything, all the money I've got is in the vase on the mantel and the food's in the dresser. If you're still here I'll see you in the morning but I don't suppose you'd get very far on a night like this.'

'Goodnight,' I said, but he only grunted and closed the stair door behind him. Then I heard a bolt being slid into place. He certainly wasn't taking any chances and I must say I didn't blame him. After all he didn't know me from a hole in the ground.

By the light of the fire I spread the blankets on the sofa and decided that when it died down I'd probably be pretty cold so I'd sleep fully dressed.

I lay on my back watching the firelight dancing across the ceiling while I thought through the events of the day. I thought about the stupidity and getting injured and lost, about my parents and what, if anything, they had done since I left. I also thought about the old man. Gruff as he was at least he'd taken me in and fed me – but tomorrow I'd have to move on, he'd made that very plain.

I'd just managed to identify the damp, musty smell coming from the blankets as honey and the scratching in the corner of the room as mice, when the whining of the wind round the house lulled me off to sleep.

Chapter 3

*T*HE scrape of a bucket across the quarry tiles woke me. I was cold and stiff. What bedclothes I'd piled on top of me lay tangled beside the sofa and my ankle was throbbing from inactivity making me feel bottom heavy, like a Kelly toy.

I looked around to find the cause of the noise and saw the old man lifting a bucket of snow onto the range! I lay still wondering if I was dreaming or if the events of yesterday had loosened my brain. I eventually decided this was reality, stretched, and caused the sofa to creak.

'Oh, you're awake at last,' he muttered as he stirred the fire into life. 'The water butt's frozen and I can't get to the well, so we'll have to make do with this.' He gave the contents of the bucket a prod with a wooden spoon. 'It's free and there's no shortage of it!'

I didn't like to ask questions, my mind was still bleary with sleep and most of my muscles, not just my ankle, I discovered, were still telling of yesterday's strenuous efforts.

'Can you cook?' he asked cocking an eyebrow.

'A bit.'

'Good. I'm going to feed the chickens. There's eggs and bacon on the dresser. Bread's on the table. I like three eggs, two rashers and a round of fried bread. You have what you like but don't burn anything. I can't abide wasted food.'

As he left a blast of cold air brought the first grey light of dawn trailing into the room. I glanced at the clock and realised it wasn't seven yet. My parents would still be asleep but this man, at least twice their age, was out greeting the dawn like a Druid performing rights at Stonehenge.

I creaked and crawled out of bed. As soon as my stockinged feet touched the ice cold tiles the reality of where I was came back to me. I grabbed my baseball boots from where they'd been baking on the range and decided to delay changing back into my own clothes until after breakfast when the place might have warmed up a bit. The contrast between this place and the centrally heated flat I was used to was giving me goose-pimples.

The cold water I flung over my face was mind straining, there was ice round the edge of the bucket, and when I cleaned my teeth it felt as if they were all naked nerves with no enamel. I glanced in the fly-blown mirror; my eye looked worse and my ankle still hurt when my foot touched ground.

Hopping around cooking eggs and bacon isn't the easiest thing in the world to do. Finding things was the first problem. The frying pan turned up on the end of the sewing machine. An old, iron one it had obviously been used for breakfast before judging by the scraps of bacon rind marooned in the congealed lard. I decided to ignore the mouseprints which looked as if they belonged to my companion of the night.

Once I'd collected everything it was easier to sit in front of the range and cook. That way I got the best advantage of the heat and had time to look around me. Last night's lamplight had blurred the detail of a room which was last papered about the end of the Second World War, the only additions being an all over abstract of smoke and damp stains as if it was in pickle. Even the paint on the woodwork was cracked and blistered and whatever colour it was originally it had settled down to a restful brown. Which things were used most often could be judged by the layer of dust they held, those least used had a coat as thick as a cat's.

The calendar on the wall just below the clock looked like the only thing that had come into the house during the last twelve months.

The old man came in through the back door with an empty

20

sack over his shoulders which was plastered with fresh snow.

'I said you couldn't stay here today,' he paused to blow on his hands, 'but it seems you can't leave.'

I'd left the curtains closed to keep whatever heat there was in the room but now he flung them back and the dull old place was full of white light.

It was still snowing hard and the whole landscape was covered in deep, undulating drifts only broken from time to time by the stark, black skeleton of a tree.

The old man's house was built nearly at the top of the hill so I was able to see the track I'd used winding up from the main road. It had been practically obliterated with snow and you could only find it by tracing the parallel lines of the hedge. At least, not hedge so much as tufts, poking up through the white blanket.

Further down the hill lay a large farmhouse which I suppose was where I'd seen the first set of lights. It was almost buried in the snow and looked like the carcase of some prehistoric monster.

I took one long look at the scene outside and realised just how lucky I was not to have become a permanent feature of it!

'You won't get anywhere in that. You'll have to wait until tomorrow. If you want the lavatory you go out of that door and follow my footsteps to the left. I've cleared some of the snow away but there's an old walking stick you can use, to steady yourself, by the door.'

Outside the wind was bitingly cold and the snow driving into my face reminded me only too strongly of my experience the previous afternoon. I could hardly believe it was less than twenty-four hours since I'd left home, so much had happened and none of it good.

I found the privy at the end of a row of broken-down outbuildings. The snow was piled up against it like an igloo. The neat squares of newspaper hanging from a nail and the scrubbed pine top were its best features!

As I picked my way back gingerly towards the house I got some idea of how lucky I'd been to find shelter the previous

21

night. Where the wind had been driving the snow into drifts against the house it was piled up to just below the bedroom window. I turned with a shudder at the thought of being underneath one of those drifts and made for the warmth, comparatively, of the house.

'You aren't a bad cook,' the old man said, a trickle of egg yolk wandering down his chin.

'I've had lots of practice.'

'We'll have to go easy on the milk,' he added as he poured us second cups of tea. I hate tea. It always tastes like wet brown paper to me. My mother's a tea-coholic. Whenever she's around there's always a full teapot close by.

'I shan't be able to get down to the farm for fresh milk today. There's some dried stuff in the cupboard but I don't much like using it. Seems against nature to me.'

The news that the snow was too deep for me to leave had made me feel much more cheerful because if I couldn't leave there was no chance of the old man sending for a doctor, who was bound to ask awkward questions. But I couldn't help thinking about home and wondering if they'd had as much snow.

Maybe I'd been a bit stupid leaving home. The trouble was I could never make Dad see reason, even if it came drawn by horses and festooned with bells. If I tried to put my point of view he just got cross and then lashed out. The other trouble was that when he did that, instead of standing up for myself I always went for the soft option and gave up.

There was no doubt he'd be hopping mad by now so there was no sense in going back. I'd be the last person he'd want to listen to. I might just as well keep going while I had the chance.

'I'd better cut some wood for the fire in case the weather turns any worse.'

'I could do that for you,' I offered.

'With that ankle? – No, I'll do it. You'd better stop in the house as much as you can. You can clear up the dishes.'

He clamped a hat on his head, threw the protective sack back over his shoulders and stomped off out of the house.

22

I used lots of boiling water on the dishes. If I was going to eat many more meals here I decided to do it off clean plates with clean cutlery. During both the meals so far I'd eaten things I thought were part of the pattern on the plate and I hadn't survived a blizzard to die of beriberi or something.

Hoping to while away the time I tried the wireless. It was a great, brown, bakelite monstrosity but it gave out only pops, bangs and high pitched whistles. I wished in a way that I'd brought my tranny but then, if we didn't have a radio it would stop the old man finding out if my Mum had gone to the police and made me a news item.

The sink was just under the window so, while I washed up, I was able to watch for signs of life in the valley. In fact the old man had a good place for watching life without being part of it. The only thing was, that on that particular day, very little seemed to be moving. I looked out for traffic moving down on the main road but I didn't even see a gritter. The snow must have been much worse than I thought.

By the time I'd finished my job it had actually stopped snowing but the wind was lifting the fallen snow and dumping it in ever changing patterns. This meant it settled against any solid object and quickly piled up behind it. It also meant that the few tracks the old man had cleared were rapidly refilled. Although the snow had fallen in small drops over a long period the wind was shifting it in bulk as efficiently as a snow plough.

I turned my back on the window. The view was beginning to depress me. I looked around for something to do. There was plenty of dust around, but I wasn't sure how to remove that without the aid of a vacuum cleaner.

A row of books caught my eye. They couldn't have been moved since Adam was a lad in short trousers, the dust was so thick and the book nearest the outside wall was welded to the plaster by green mould.

One of the books, *The Adventures of Tom Sawyer*, was one that everyone went on about but I'd never read. I pulled it out and riffled the pages which were yellow with damp and ploughed by worm. As two airmail envelopes slipped from between the

23

leaves and drifted to the ground the back door flew open.

'Put those back!' he shouted. He stood framed in the doorway, his arms full of logs. Cold and anger made the veins on his face stand out as vividly as roads on a map. 'They're none of your business.'

'I'm sorry, I wasn't prying,' I apologised as I snatched up the letters and stuffed them back inside the cover.

The old man didn't speak but nudged the door to with his elbow and then arranged the logs on the range with studied care.

'Listen,' he said at last, 'I don't know who you are, what you've done, or why you're not at home where you should be.'

He took the book from me and pushed his face close. 'All I do know is, that while you're under my roof you keep yourself and your nose out of my affairs. And then, when you leave here, you don't tell anyone where you've been. Is that clear?'

I nodded, taken aback by his severity.

'As long as that's understood. No names, nothing. I don't want to know your name and you aren't going to know mine. Just, when you go, forget you ever met me, and I'll do the same for you.'

'Thanks.'

He turned away and busied himself around the range while I withdrew to the sofa to tidy up my belongings. I was puzzled by what he'd said. It sounded as if there was something about me which threatened him and I thought the boot was on the other foot. He only had to report me to the police and I was finished.

I was sure that he wasn't afraid of me attacking him; old as he was I could see that he'd put up a struggle and make a good account of himself. Nobody would get into his house unless he said so! Unlike Dad who would probably offer them a drink.

Although his temper flared quickly it died away equally fast and by the time we sat down for our midday meal he was chatting quite amiably about what he grew in the garden and so on. He seemed to enjoy it but it sounded like hard work of a kind I could never get used to. Stuck out here all your life with cabbages and chickens for company.

In the afternoon the wind got up and it started to snow heavily again. He went out to clear the paths but soon gave it up as a losing battle and by four o'clock we were glad to pull the curtains and light the lamp.

We had so little in common that the chat ran dry by the evening and he rummaged round until he found a pack of playing cards and he taught me a version of mock-whist. He didn't explain the rules very well, in fact I think he made some of them up to suit the situation, so it wasn't surprising that he won nearly every hand. It was even less surprising when I discovered that there were six cards missing from the pack and he knew perfectly well which six!

When he went up to bed that night I was quite surprised that he didn't bother to bolt the door. He wasn't expecting to get his throat slit in the night any more. But he did take the copy of *Tom Sawyer* up with him, which I thought was odd until I realised that those letters probably had his name and address written on them and, after what he'd said, he'd rather I didn't know what that was.

I fell asleep that night with mixed feelings. In some ways I would have been glad to be able to get on my way, but, if I had to be stuck anywhere it might just as well be here. At least the old man wasn't poking his nose into my affairs, in fact it was perfectly clear that he would heave a big sigh of relief when I left, though why that was I couldn't work out.

Chapter 4

*T*HERE was no sound in the house when I woke up. Through a chink in the curtains light was shining into the room but the fire lay dead in the grate and I was frozen! The clock on the wall showed that it was after eight, the old man had been up long before this yesterday.

Throwing on every article of clothing I could find, including my anorak and a blanket round my shoulders, I ran over to the fire. I knew that if he had overslept the last thing he'd want to come down to would be a dead fire and a cold wind.

My first attempt wasn't an enormous success. Clouds of black smoke went up the chimney only to return and fill the room, leaving me choking and rubbing my eyes. Living in a centrally heated flat hadn't equipped me for this job.

Draught! That was the answer. I unbolted the door and flung it open in the hope that there would be sufficient breeze to reverse the draught in the flue. There was, more than enough. Bright flames appeared in the grate and the smoke went dutifully up the chimney.

All I had to do now was clear the ton of snow which had fallen into the kitchen when I opened the door! I hadn't realised how bad the drifting had been during the night and in fact it was still snowing. Great flakes of the stuff flew past me into the room but the door was firmly jammed with snow and I couldn't close it until that was shifted with the aid of the coal shovel.

I did that as fast as I could in case the old man should come

26

down and see what a stupid mistake I'd made and how much mess it had left, but even when I'd finished there was no sign of him and no sound of movement upstairs.

I made a pot of lukewarm tea, which I had to drink black because the milk had run out the previous night, and considered the position. It was perfectly possible that he'd decided to have a lie in but my limited experience told me that that was unlikely on two counts. Firstly, old people tend to be creatures of habit, that way they know where they are. They appear to have milestones in the day and they mark them off as they pass. Secondly, their bladders don't allow them to lie in bed late. Which reminded me that it was time I braved the elements.

When I came back, older, wiser and a good deal colder and there was still no sign of movement I really began to worry.

Suppose he was lying upstairs, dead? But then, suppose he was lying upstairs ill? It was nearly nine o'clock and I decided that whatever the old man said if I disturbed him I wasn't going to risk waiting any longer. I'd rather he was furious with me than suffering up there on his own.

I opened the stairs-door and went slowly up the steep, uncarpeted, wooden steps. By the time I got to the third one, I was wondering what I was going to do if I had to stay in the house alone with a dead body! At least there was no shortage of snow to pack it in outside. I shivered now with more than just the cold air of the staircase.

At the head of the stairs there were three doors, all painted with the same blistered brown as downstairs, and all firmly closed. The skylight was covered in snow and only let through a dim, bluish light.

I tried the door to the left. The room was totally empty except for a brass bedstead with no mattress. The air was cold and the windows had thick frost patterns on the inside.

The room to the right was just as cold and empty. Across the vast desert of faded linoleum a wormy washstand leant unsteadily against the wall and a pair of flowery curtains, overpatterned with the brown stains of damp, hung dejectedly at the windows.

I stood out on the landing for a moment, knowing that the

answers to all my questions lay behind the third door. I took a deep breath and pressed the black latch. The door creaked open.

'Hello?' I said softly, but there was no reply.

The room was in darkness, the curtains were still closed and I was only able to make out dim shapes by the light from the landing. Then I heard a quiet sort of moan, or it could have been just a snore.

Frightened and relieved at one and the same time I threw open the curtains and turned to see the old man lying in a narrow iron bedstead which was piled so high with coats, pullovers and blankets that he was hardly visible.

I eased the sheets back from his face. His skin was almost translucent beneath its tan and there was no movement or twitch of any kind. Perhaps he was dead after all. I didn't fancy grubbing around a dead body looking for a pulse but then I remembered what they always did in films, hold a mirror up to the face to see if there's any sign of breath! Not very scientific, but what else could I do?

There wasn't a mirror in the room and I was just about to run down and collect the one from the kitchen when he moaned. I was very relieved. Not only that he'd moaned, which proved he was still alive, but that he'd done it before I'd collected the mirror. I would never have been able to explain what I was doing standing over him with a mirror in my hand.

A film of sweat stood out on his forehead and he opened his eyes and muttered something that sounded like, 'Fine mess!' then he closed his eyes again. Despite the mound of clothes on the bed he was shivering quite violently. I looked round and saw a small grate set in the wall. It hadn't been used for ages by the look of it but if I could light a fire the room might warm up a little. Warmth was obviously what he needed.

To be honest I hadn't a clue what he needed, or what was wrong with him for that matter, but I did know there was no way I could get across the snow for help and I was less likely to panic while I was active.

Within half an hour I'd lit a fire, made some fresh tea, cut him

28

some thin bread and butter and my ankle was aching like fury again from all the running up and down stairs.

The fire worked, when I'd propped him up a little so did the tea, but the bread and butter lay on the plate curling at the edges. As the room warmed up he opened his eyes occasionally but it seemed ages before he spoke again.

'Corn,' he said in a thin, asthmatic croak.

I just looked at him foolishly. I hadn't a clue what he was talking about but it was obviously important to him.

'Corn,' he said again. 'For the chickens.'

This time I got the message. 'Don't worry, I'll look after them,' I said, giving him a grin which was supposed to inspire confidence.

I went downstairs with some misgivings. The only chickens I'd ever had anything to do with came home naked in plastic bags at Christmas or only had legs, and were served with a portion of chips.

I had to find them first anyway. I shovelled valiantly at snow drifts outside the outbuildings. I unearthed, in order, the toolshed, the wood store, and what looked like a pigsty. Fortunately this was vacant although there were tangible signs of fairly recent occupation. I doubt if I could have coped with a pig when I couldn't even find the chickens.

Snow was still falling. As it melted on my back and shoulders then seeped straight through to my skin I began to realise why the old man put a sack across his shoulders.

I shovelled away at the last possible door and, as usually happens on these occasions, found that my last choice was the correct one! As I flung open the door, through a flurry of dust and feathers, I saw hens.

To be honest when he'd said 'chickens' I'd been expecting the little, fluffy, yellow things that the people who design Easter cards are so fond of, not full grown hens. It shows just how much I knew about the countryside because, of course, I'd been eating their eggs!

The next problem was feeding them. I know he'd said corn but he'd forgotten that I lived in a city. To me corn was tall, yellow stuff that waved about in the sunshine, or came in flakes and you put milk on them. It's funny how you learn all sorts of stuff at school but you don't think it affects you, so you don't take a great deal of notice. Mind you, knowing which countries grow it and how much wasn't going to help me find a bucket of it.

Eventually I found a sack of seed that looked the right sort of thing. I filled the bucket with it, emptied it on the chicken house floor and to my relief, corn or not, they started pecking at it as hard as they could go.

Then I noticed their drinker which was frozen solid. I took that back to the house and put it on the range to thaw while I had a look at the old man and another cup of black, horrible tea.

When I took the water back to the hens I was glad to see that they weren't all lying on their backs with their feet in the air. With a sense of accomplishment I shut the door and wandered back to the house. Only then did I remember that I hadn't eaten yet and it was almost midday. With the old man safely upstairs I did the biggest fry-up you've ever seen and ate my way steadily through it while I wondered what sort of food I could give him.

Soup seemed the best answer and when I took it up for him he obviously agreed. I propped him up with extra pillows but he couldn't manage the mug himself so I fed him off a spoon and he took the stuff with great slurps.

He'd drunk about half of it when he gently pushed the mug away.

'Thanks lad,' he murmured then closed his eyes and peacefully dozed off to sleep.

With the old man safely asleep upstairs I decided to see if I could get the battered old wireless to work. I was quite anxious to hear a weather forecast because as soon as the snow stopped I'd probably be moving on.

Being used to a transistor that starts as soon as you turn the switch I'd almost given this up for lost when suddenly it emitted a series of crackling pops. By sticking my ear to the loudspeaker I was just able to tune it but of course I should have realised that the clock was wrong, I'd missed the forecast. I decided to listen to the news, which had already started, because they might have something to say about the weather.

After the usual run down of trouble in Africa, increase in jobless totals for the month, strikes in the car industry and an increase in the price of petrol they got round to the weather. Apparently deep snow was covering most of the country from Scotland right down to the South West and the Midlands was pretty badly hit according to them.

They got reporters from all over the place each giving a local story. A shepherd in Scotland had rescued thirteen new born lambs from under a ten foot snow drift, some people who'd been stuck in a café on the Snake Pass had spent the night playing cards and the snow had made one man £300 richer. Then they got to the Midlands and I nearly fell out of my chair.

'Midlands police are continuing their search for the missing seventeen-year-old boy who left home at the start of the blizzard and hasn't been seen now for three days. Peter Simpson's mother appealed, today, for the boy to get in touch if he's safe. Peter, who's five foot eight, with brown collar length hair and brown eyes, is thought to be wearing a reddish anorak, and jeans, and may be carrying a duffel bag. Anyone with any information should contact their nearest police station.'

I snapped the wireless off feeling very peculiar. I couldn't help feeling a small glow of pride at being mentioned on the news but it also made me wonder what my mates were thinking. Running away from home was one thing, but getting lost in the snow wasn't very impressive.

Then there was my mother. I felt a bit choked about her. When I got to Manchester I was going to ring up and say I was all right so that she wouldn't worry. I'd left a note saying I was going but that wasn't enough. Now I couldn't do anything, I was powerless stuck out here. It was obvious the police thought I was dead so probably that's what Mum and Dad thought too! That wasn't what I'd had in mind when I'd left home.

Because I didn't know how much longer he was going to stay

31

upstairs I took the precaution of disconnecting a couple of wires in the radio. Much as I would have liked to keep an ear open to see what happened next I thought it better that he didn't hear.

I forget which day it was I first saw the snow-ploughs down on the main road. I was washing my shirt through and looking down into the valley to see two yellow monsters spewing great clouds of snow up into the air off the road. At first they looked like intruders and I resented their appearance on the bleak, white landscape but when they showed no inclination to come up the lane towards the cottage that feeling subsided. Instead I quite enjoyed watching the trickle of traffic which followed, enjoying the sensation that I could see them although they couldn't see me.

I suppose really it was all a bit childish but I almost felt like one of those Western Outlaws you read about. The bounty hunters were out looking for me and all the time I just hid up in a cave and watched.

In fact the 'cave' was beginning to get on my nerves. It was one thing to be hidden away, safe, but it was another to be a prisoner. The constant snow made it impossible to do anything more than struggle round the few paths between the outbuildings. My ankle was much stronger and I made it my business to keep those paths clear. For one thing it was a way of getting out into the fresh air. There was little chance of me being spotted because the snow was so deep that the paths ran in a series of shoulder high trenches, but they only increased the feeling of being shut in.

That news item I'd heard was very much on my mind. If it was on the radio then no doubt the newspapers and television would use the story as well, and they had pictures, they always do with missing people. I knew exactly which picture too!

It was my Mum's favourite. She always kept it on the television next to the Spanish Dancer table lamp. When I was about six I remember lifting the Dancer's skirt to see if she was wearing knickers only to find out that she hadn't even got legs, just a brass rod. I'd asked Mum if she'd move the lamp and the photograph many a time. I found them both cringe-makingly embarrassing. The photo made me look as if I'd had my mind removed and the thought of that being flashed across the nation and appearing on every breakfast table in the country made my stomach heave. It was enough in itself to send me into permanent hiding.

During the next two or three days the hens stopped laying, the weather got worse and the old man started to recover.

'I'd like to move downstairs,' he announced one morning over early morning tea. I'd long since given up the vile stuff and just drank cold water but he still drank it.

'Into the kitchen?'

'You could put my bed in the parlour,' he suggested and I quite liked the idea because the door was kept locked and I hadn't had a chance to see in there yet. 'I could get up for a bit then, as long as I didn't have to keep going up and down those stairs. I'm not used to having people wait on me hand and foot.'

I was delighted with the idea because with any luck it might mean I would get taken off chamber pot duty. Until the old man was taken ill I thought those things were only used as joke plant pot holders, or for rich Americans to put on their bars full of ice.

Getting him down didn't turn out all that easy. He'd thought his legs were stronger than they were and eventually he came down a step at a time on his bottom. It seemed to take for ever and when he was finally down he sat on the sofa, looking pretty washed out, while I brought his bed down.

He produced the key and the parlour door lock reluctantly turned over. Judging by the little walnut tables and the tall glass-fronted bureau this room had at one time been somebody's pride and joy, but the damp had taken the bloom off the polished surfaces and their veneers were peeling up like dried out spaghetti.

I lit a fire as soon as I'd made up the bed to try and get rid of the musty, damp air which hung over the room. The old man was more anxious to get back into bed than anything else, he was still tired from the journey downstairs and that night we ate our meal in there.

'Me Mam's pride and joy this room was,' he cast a baleful eye

33

over the damp-stained antimacassars. 'She'd have wept to see it like this.'

'Have you always lived here?'

'No, we came when I was small though. Dad lost his job when the old Master died but he got the chance of one up here. The only trouble was it was two hundred miles and we had to make the journey by cart.'

'Horse and cart?'

'No other way. My Uncle was a carter and he helped Dad pile everything we owned on the cart. Mam sat in that old rocking chair all the way here and I was stuffed in amongst the buckets and brooms with my brother, when I wasn't trying to get a ride on the horse. Folks along the way thought we were tinkers. I remember one village, they wouldn't let us stop the night, they set the dogs on us!'

'Two hundred miles – how long did it take?'

'Best part of a fortnight. Most exciting time of my life I reckon! I never wanted to sleep in a house again after that. We all slept on straw under the cart with a horse blanket thrown over us. If ever I smell a horse I always think back to those nights out under the stars.'

It made my own inept journey sound pretty tame by comparison. 'They were hard times weren't they?'

'We didn't know any different then and we were glad enough of the chance of a job. If my Dad had been a single man he'd have walked it. As it was my Uncle still had to make the journey back again but he wasn't out of pocket. All the way up here he'd lit on jobs he could do on the way back. He said he might do it as a regular thing but he didn't, too lazy. No, I'll never forget the first sight of this valley. The sun was coming up over the shoulder of the hill and there it was spread out before us. Looked like the promised land!'

I can't say that I had quite the same rosy view of the place as that. To me it was the back of beyond and apart from anything else food was running short.

I suppose being used to bad winters he had a fairly good stock of food and kept sacks of things like flour and potatoes but meat was certainly becoming a problem. Most of it came out of tins, many of which were rusty and had lost their labels. The whole thing became a bit of a lottery, never knowing whether you were opening pudding or a main dish. Not only that but his principle was that food was too good and too expensive to waste, so once a tin was open we ate it whatever it was. One day we had tinned peaches followed by tinned prunes and finished off with prunes. I spent the next day shivering in the privy, which was itself becoming something of a problem that I still shudder to think about.

I suppose we wouldn't have starved to death or anything so dramatic because he had jars of honey and preserves but the diet, like the life itself, was getting very monotonous.

Stupid things got very annoying. He had a very odd way of sticking his finger in his ear and stirring it round like a spoon which I'd never noticed when I first arrived but I began to think that if he did it once more I'd go right out of my mind! I'm sure he felt the same about me too, it was the problem of being stuck in there together for so long.

I was lying on the sofa one morning wondering if I ought to get up (and if so what for?) when the old man came shuffling into the room with a blanket wrapped round him.

'Can you hear anything?' he asked.

I listened. 'Nothing special.'

'Can't you hear water dripping?'

I jumped off the sofa and we went over to the window together.

'I think there's a bit of a thaw,' he said and threw back the curtain. The sun had broken through the cloud and a steady drip of water from the roof was passing in front of the window. 'I think the worst's over.'

Chapter 5

'I'D just like to say, I'm grateful for what you've done,' the old man managed to mumble. I think he felt as awkward saying it as I was embarrassed to hear him. I always hate being praised, I never know what to do. I can never accept it and if you disagree it seems rude. Mind you, it's never been a problem I've had to face at home.

'Forget it,' I mumbled back ungraciously.

'If it hadn't been for you, I'd probably have been a gonner.'

We were on our way to see why the chickens had stopped laying. It was the first time he'd been out since his illness. Although the thaw had set in, and the pathways had turned to water, the deeper snow, he told me, would take ages to melt away. It was topped with a glossy surface from re-freezing overnight.

'I've known snow like this lie until Easter,' he said as we walked very slowly down the narrow trench. 'It melts from the bottom.'

I opened the door of the henhouse and there was a flurry of feathers just like the first time I'd seen them, only this time there was no flapping of wings. A forlorn huddle of fat birds stood at the end of the shed.

'If ever you reckon to make a fortune,' he said, rubbing his stubbly chin, 'I wouldn't be a poultry farmer.'

'What did I do wrong?'

'Hen's need light as well as food. Don't they teach you anything at school these days?' he shifted a hook that let a wooden ventilator slide down to admit a drift of weak sunlight into the shed which made the hens blink.

I didn't explain that looking after hens wasn't part of the G.C.E. O-Level syllabus, I just stood there feeling stupid.

'They've gone into moult. That's why they aren't laying. We'll be lucky if they start laying again.'

'I thought they'd be all right with food and water.'

'It's not your fault. I should have remembered you were a townie. Any kid round here would have known. Still, at least they haven't starved to death, they look like footballs.'

'I've been giving them corn like you said.'

'All the time? – just corn?'

I nodded.

'I'll show you what to do tomorrow. Let's go back to the house now, I still feel the cold out here.'

When we got back just that short walk had tired him out and he slumped gratefully into a chair by the fire while I made yet another pot of tea. If ever I see snow now I always think about those interminable cups of tea and just the smell is enough, to this day I can't drink a cup, even with milk.

'You remember, before I was taken bad, I said you had to go the next day?'

I nodded. This was the moment I'd been dreading. I didn't even really know what I wanted him to say next.

'The way I was I wouldn't have blamed you if you'd taken me at me word and cleared off. There's plenty that would. I want you to realise I appreciate what you did for me. But what are you going to do now? I'm better, the roads are clear. Are you still off to Manchester?'

What I knew of course was that every policeman in the country knew what I looked like and if I set foot on the main road it wouldn't be very long before I was spotted, picked up and taken home.

'The choice is yours,' the old man said. 'I don't have the slightest idea of what you're up to and I don't want to. All I'm saying is, I'm grateful for what you did and if you want to stay here a bit longer, you can.'

'I'd like to stay,' I said quickly. Things would quieten down and people would forget I was missing, then I could get moving again in safety. Maybe another couple of weeks would do it. 'Just for a bit longer.'

'There is one condition. That you write a note to your parents. You don't have to say where you are or anything, just that you're all right.'

'O.K.' It was easy to agree. I'd always meant to do that and, although I knew that it would stir the hunt up again so that I might have to wait a little longer before leaving, I'd rather that than have Mum thinking I was dead.

'I'll post it when I next go down to the shop,' he said and sat back relieved that it was all over.

The rasp of a heel in the yard spun my head round. It was quickly followed by a thump on the door. I leapt out of my seat and was making for the parlour door when the old man stopped me.

'It'll only be Mr Bailey from the farm. Odd he hasn't been up 'til now,' he turned towards the door. 'Come in Charlie, it's not locked.'

The door swung open and a great barn of a man instantly filled the room.

'Hello, Moses,' he boomed out. 'You didn't come down for your milk so I thought I'd best come up and see. The wife's sent over some things.'

He dumped the milk container on the table and then proceeded, like some giant conjuror, to produce packets, tins and bottles from every pocket using hands that looked like table tennis bats.

'We knew you were all right,' he said after the last pocket was emptied. 'Looked for your smoke each day. The missus watches your chimney like an Indian waiting for a message.'

For all his size he seemed a shy man. He'd noticed me as soon as he'd come through the door but he didn't say anything. Until now he'd just shot the occasional glance at me out of the corner

38

of his eye, the way you look at someone you don't know well enough to tell them their zip's undone.

'Didn't realise you had visitors,' he shifted from foot to foot his vast boots scratching two years life expectancy out of the tiles every time he moved.

'Friend of mine,' the old man said, 'he's stopping a while. Sit down Charlie, the lad will pour us some tea.'

Charlie shoved himself into a chair like a double-decker bus backing into a garage. The chair creaked in protest and screeched backwards across the quarry tiles as if it was trying to escape from the unreasonable load.

I poured them mugs of tea but I had a mug of fresh, creamy milk. I'd never tasted milk fresh from the cow and nothing since has ever tasted as good as it did that day.

'Stopping long?' Charlie Bailey asked.

'Just a while,' the old man said before I could answer. He tapped the side of his nose with a finger and winked. 'No questions, no lies. As a matter of fact, if it hadn't been for this young chap, you wouldn't have been talking to me now.'

'Taken bad again?'

'Aye,' the old man sounded scornful of himself.

'Your old trouble? – I've told you about living in this damp old place. Ought to get yourself out of this place and into one of those nice bungalows they're putting up in the village.'

'I'd sooner be in my box than in one of those,' the old man spat contemptuously into the fire.

It was obviously a topic they'd discussed hundreds of times before. Mr Bailey just grinned to himself and shook his head at the old man. Their attention shifted to the weather.

'Bad this time.'

'Nearly as bad as forty-seven. I couldn't get the milk out for a few days. Just had to chuck it down the drain.'

I thought bitterly of the milkless days we'd spent up here, unable to get to the farm, while they were pouring the stuff away and I was drinking black tea.

'They're still cut off in parts of Scotland and Devon,' Charlie went on. 'Still I expect you've heard all about it on the wireless?'

39

'Wireless is broke.'

'Oh!' said Charlie knowingly, 'there's a lot you'll have missed then!'

He shot a look in my direction and I felt myself turn bright scarlet. With my fading black eye and bruised nose I must have been a colourful sight. Like a damaged beetroot.

'Nothing I needed to know,' the old man said quietly.

In the silence that followed, Charlie's great hands fluttered nervously around the side pockets as if he might yet produce a pair of white doves or a rabbit.

'So, you were bad?' he said at last. 'You're all right now though?'

'Just need a bit more rest. I'll be down in a couple of days.'

'No need for that. It's too wet to do much. You're sure there's nothing we can get you? Nothing from the chemist, I know you won't see the doctor?'

'I'm all right. How's the snow in the bottom meadow?'

They fell into a long discussion about mole drains, leasows and hoggets that lost me completely, then Charlie Bailey suddenly started to heave himself out of his chair. He flung his great hand on to the table like a slab of raw meat sending the bottles and jars quivering noisily in fright.

'Anyway, I thought I'd just call, make sure you were all right. The missus worries about you.'

'You tell her I'm all right, and she's not to worry.'

'I'll tell her.'

'And I'll be down to settle for those groceries.'

'We know you won't run off.'

'I like to be straight.'

'You get yourself straight first,' Mr Bailey backed towards the door as he spoke, almost as if the old man was royalty, and I began to wonder if his great bulk would go crashing backwards through the door. Neither of the two men seemed to know how to break the conversation off. In the end Mr Bailey lifted his hand to the old man, gave me a curt nod and left without ever actually saying goodbye.

'He knows who I am,' I said as soon as the door was shut. I

40

started to stack away the groceries. I was delighted to see there was a small jar of coffee and the old chap was equally pleased to see a tin of tobacco.

'Maybe he does,' he said as he reached for his pipe, 'but he won't say anything to anyone. It's my business who I have up here. Country folk aren't like town folk. They like to know what's going on but that doesn't mean they'll blab it all over the place. I said you're stopping with me for a bit and that'll do for Charlie Bailey.'

'I hope you're right.'

'I know I am. If you're stopping we'd better have some names now. You heard Charlie call me Moses? Moses Beech. You call me Moses, everybody calls me Moses. Only strangers call me Mister Beech. And what do I call you?'

'Pete.'

'Right.'

Having names for each other seemed to make life suddenly a whole lot easier and more secure in a way.

'Unusual name, Moses.'

'Might be these days but when I was born people got everything out of the Bible, including names. My name's in the Bible in more ways than one. Get it out of the parlour.'

I'd noticed the great heavy book when I'd been nursing Moses but I knew better than to touch anything without his say-so. When I put it down on the kitchen table Moses undid the brass clasps and showed me the family photographs that were pasted into the front, each with a name written beneath in spidery, black copperplate.

'That's my brother Enoch,' he said pointing to a lad in a sailor suit. 'And this one's Joseph.'

'Do they still live around here?'

'Enoch died when he was still a baby. Mam was carrying him when we came here on the cart. She reckoned he was weak because of it, I don't know. Joseph was younger than me. He broke Mam's heart. He said there was nothing for him round here, said he was going to Australia.'

Looking at the small, oval sepia print of a little boy with blond curls it was hard to imagine him grown up and running away from home. All the same I felt a certain fellow feeling for him. When your life seems dull and suffocating it's a great temptation to just jump over the wall. I wondered if the airmail envelopes I'd found came from Joseph but thought better of asking.

'Didn't you ever want to leave here?'

He hesitated for a moment. 'No, not really.'

'Have you never been away from here at all?'

'I go in to market in the summer, that's more than enough for me.'

'Cities are all right. I'd miss the cinemas and the discos. Have you never even been away for a holiday?'

'Holiday?' he laughed so much he choked on his pipe. 'You young 'uns don't know you're born! I was a cowman. Cows need milking twice a day, seven days a week, high days and holidays. Nowadays they get relief men in if the farmer won't do it himself. I was glad of the money. There were plenty of people who didn't know where their next meal was coming from.'

'You look well dressed in those photographs.'

'Aye, and I'll bet you a pound to a penny that I could take you round ten or twenty cottages in the village and they'd all have photographs of themselves in those same clothes.'

'Weren't they your clothes?'

'No,' Moses spat scornfully into the fire. 'Came from the vicarage and when you outgrew them they went back for somebody else. You get everything handed to you on a plate these days and you still want more.'

I'd worn second-hand clothes for most of my life and I certainly didn't share Moses' view. I was only too glad when we moved into the council flat which was too far away from the old clothes shop Mum used to patronize. It wasn't the clothes I minded so much, Mum soon found her way to Oxfam anyway, but the old man with the dirty hands who ran it.

'Who were you a cowman for?'

'The Squire, same as me father. Only with Dad it was horses. Squire was a great hunting man and he bred horses as a hobby.

42

That's why he particularly wanted my Dad and that's why I own
this house now.'

'You mean you bought it, or your Dad did?'

'Neither of us. Never saw the money that would have bought
this place,' he settled back into his chair with pride as he started on
his tale. 'I said the Squire bred horses. He had this favourite mare
of his and she had a difficult foaling. Vets all come and shook their
heads, reckoned it was all up with her and they should put her out
of her misery with a shot-gun. But Dad said he'd see her through.
He never left her side. Ate his meals and slept in the stable.
Anyway mare had her foal and the Squire was tickled pink. What
do you think he said to Dad?'

'I don't know.'

'Nothing, not a word!'

'I bet your Dad was sore.'

'Maybe he was, but he didn't let on. After all, he'd only done his
job, hadn't he?'

'The Squire might have shown a bit of gratitude.'

'Well, he died a few years later and he left this place to Dad in
his Will. It said, "In recognition of devotion above the average".'

'Why didn't he just give it to your Dad while he was still alive?'

'Two reasons. Dad knew his place and if the Squire had just
given him the property they wouldn't have known how to face
each other; but second, he wanted to show Dad it was something
he'd never forgotten right up to the day he died.'

Chapter 6

'You'll see a stile at the end of the garden,' Moses said. It was half-past seven and still not light but Moses was anxious to get out. This was his first day back at work.

'There's a path skirting the wood, the well's a couple of hundred yards down there. There used to be a well right by the house but it dried up. Charlie Bailey wanted to bring me the stuff up in churns on his tractor but the stuff they drink down there doesn't taste right to me.'

'They've got mains water?' I asked, trying to sound alert and interested despite the fact I was half asleep and only half-way through my breakfast.

'Yes,' he said in tones of absolute disgust. 'I don't know what they put in it but I can't stand the taste of it.'

'Why didn't you have the mains brought up here? You could wash in it at least.'

'There's enough water lands on the roof to wash in, I've always washed in rainwater, so did Mam. I wouldn't let them bring their mains up here.'

Moses got up, collected his sandwich box and walked over to the door.

'Don't forget to collect the milk,' he said, and with that he was gone.

It really puzzled me that Moses went out to work at all at his age but his eagerness to get there before the crack of dawn astonished me even more. When he and Charlie Bailey had talked about it before I'd assumed that Moses just went down to do odd jobs, now it seemed as though it was a full time occupation.

I finished my breakfast quickly, more out of guilt than anything else, and started to clear up. We'd agreed that I should live rent free, which was perhaps as well because most of my small savings was in my Post Office book and I wouldn't have been able to get that out without the whole world knowing exactly where I was. In exchange I was to do the cooking and housework.

I suppose that might have bothered a lot of the boys at school but with Mum being Queen of the Bingo Halls and Dad having a full time job swinging the Social Security payments I'd spent a good deal of my life looking after that sort of thing.

'I wonder why I don't mind doing it out here when I always grumbled because I had to do it at home?' I asked myself as I ran the rag Moses had found over the breakfast plates. The washing up cloth was his only concession to hygiene and I reckon any Health Department would have condemned it on sight, or at least smell. However it was a big step forward on his old method which was to use one plate for all the meals on any one day and if the last meal had lots of gravy he would clean that up with his bread and consider it ready for breakfast!

As I rinsed the cups the first morning light came up behind the opposite side of the valley. The cars and lorries down on the main road switched off their lights one by one. The broad sweep of the valley, still in its winter green and brown, only occasionally broken by the odd drift of snow which still lay in the shadow of a wall or tree, looked really great. I told myself that was why I didn't mind things so much out here. It beat looking out of the twelfth storey window of our high rise flat from which all I ever got was vertigo.

When I'd finished tidying the house inside I put on my anorak, and an old pair of Wellington boots Moses had found for me, to go and feed the chickens.

Outside the air was crisp and fresh, the traffic on the main road was too little and too far away for the fumes to affect the

45

cottage. The chickens and I had developed what can only be called a working relationship. They laid the occasional egg, I left them alone and they still eyed me with a certain amount of mistrust.

I collected the water buckets next and set out over the old wooden stile at the bottom of the garden. This was my first real journey since I'd arrived at the house and I felt curiously exposed up here on the side of a hill. Anybody who glanced up could easily see me walking along the path just below the wood. It felt like walking down the street without clothes until I told myself they'd need to be looking through a telescope to make out any detail. Then I worried about bird-watchers and astronomers, until I persuaded myself that they'd probably be a bit thin on the ground out here.

As I walked along the well beaten path the sun was just lifting the damp air out of the wood and it hung in a mist like smoke around the tops of the pine trees. Their rich scent hung in my nostrils. It reminded me of the disinfectant my mother rarely used in the bathroom and if I hadn't reached the well at that point I think I might have got homesick. I just wasn't used to all this open space and being a dot on the landscape.

Then as I walked back to the house, trying to arrive with at least some water still in the buckets, I began to worry about who might be in the house waiting for me. Moses never locked the house up when he went out.

'It's so long since I last locked it,' he said when I asked him about this, 'that I can't remember where I put the key.'

Which was fine for Moses, who had the stairs door he could bolt, but left me sleeping exposed to any passing maniac or werewolf. He'd promised me he'd find a mattress so that I could sleep in one of the upstairs rooms but he still hadn't got round to it.

The buckets had felt light when I left the well but by the time I reached the stile (although they were emptier because I'd spilt about a quarter of the contents) they felt like ton weights. My arms felt as if they were being wrenched out of their sockets and I had two broad red weals across my fingers. If Dad had asked

46

me to walk to the corner shop for two buckets of water I expect I'd have refused, but out here, despite the weals, it seemed quite fun. Almost like being on holiday. Not that I'd ever been on a holiday, we had all our rows at home.

My fears were groundless. There was nobody sitting in the house waiting to arrest me and I stowed away the two water buckets, more than willing to admit that Moses must be a good deal tougher than he looked.

The next journey was down to the farm to collect the milk and I must admit I had a cup of coffee to strengthen my nerve before I set out on that one. Apart from Moses (and the brief visit of Charlie Bailey) I hadn't spoken to anyone since the blizzard. Even though the Baileys knew all about me it still felt odd going to meet them on their own territory.

Walking down the high sided, sandy lane was pleasant enough. It was difficult to remember how different it had seemed coming up in the blizzard or how frightened I'd been when everything now seemed so calm, peaceful and ordinary. In many ways I was beginning to envy Moses his life out here. He never had to worry about catching a bus, queuing in shops or doing exams. I knew he'd left school at thirteen and he didn't seem any the worse for it. He led a very simple life with each day making its own demands. Maybe he didn't know anything about television, bingo or space travel but he didn't seem to miss them either.

As I got to the turning off towards the farm at first I laughed at myself for having missed it in the dark when it was so obvious but then the feeling of apprehension returned at the thought of meeting people. By the time I reached the farmhouse, its pink sandstone glowing in the wintry sunlight, I was almost too nervous to knock, but eventually I did. The sound echoed through the house and died away. Apart from some sparrows leaving the ivy covered walls at high speed and a cow mooing in a barn somewhere, nothing else happened. The warm smell of cows and manure surrounded me like a blanket, but still nobody came.

I was just about to take advantage of the situation, leave the milk can for Moses to bring back, and beat a hasty retreat when an apparition came round the corner of the building.

'They're out,' it said.

If she hadn't spoken I wouldn't have guessed it was a girl. A vast, tattered, shapeless jacket almost reached the knees of her equally voluminous jeans which in turn were stuffed into a huge pair of wellies. The outfit was topped off with a battered, greasy trilby which had a hen feather stuck in the band and was crammed firmly down over what little showed of her blonde hair. Her clothes and face were daubed with cow muck and she was peering at me through glasses the size of saucers. Apart from that she was straight out of *Honey*.

'I was just mucking out the cows,' she said.

'I didn't think you were cooking,' I replied, trying to get upwind of her.

'Do you want something or did you just feel like a good stare?'

'Milk,' I said, producing the can from behind my back.

'That's what I thought,' she said, grabbing the can and stomping off in her size 109 wellies. After she'd gone she seemed to leave a yellow haze of gas behind her and although she had a head start I had no difficulty in tracking her down by scent like a bloodhound. I know the theory is any girl's better than none but this one looked as if she'd mugged Worzel Gummidge.

When I reached the cool, white silence of the dairy she was just pouring the creamy-white, frothy milk into my can with a stainless steel dipper. I waited awkwardly for her to finish.

'How are you getting on with Moses?' she asked without looking up.

'All right,' I mumbled. For some reason I'd never been able to relax and just talk to girls. The other boys at school never seemed to have any difficulty but I always seemed to seize up like an unoiled machine. I may not be Robert Redford but I'm not Quasimodo either and yet girls never had any difficulty in ignoring me, because I never let them know I was even there.

'He's a nice old man,' she offered.

'Yes,' I said. Kicking myself but at the same time telling myself there was no point in getting steamed up about this refugee from a jumble sale who's blue eyes, through those goggles, looked like a fish's. She, on the other hand, seemed persistent. Maybe she was even shorter of company than I was, which wasn't surprising; probably underneath that outfit she had a figure like a barn.

'Where do you come from?'

'The Potteries,' I said reluctantly, although it was perfectly clear from the way she asked the question that she already knew the answer.

'Staying long?'

'Not very.' I was anxious to get away but she was still holding on to the milk can with her great mucky paws.

'What do you do up there all day?'

'Look after the house and things,' I was determined to be evasive, I wasn't going to tell any girl I was also going to do the cooking.

'Don't you get bored?'

'It makes a change,' I tried to sound like a playboy who's opted out of the social whirl.

'Are you still at school?'

'Does it look like it?' I tried to be as withering as possible. Hard up as I might be for company around my own age I just wasn't interested. Even if she did have a nice mouth and white teeth.

She admitted defeat and handed me the milk-can. I thanked her and turned to go.

'Don't forget the papers!' She handed me a roll of newspapers tied up with orange plastic binder twine which was lying inside the dairy door.

I thanked her again, fell over my feet, nearly spilt the milk and left hastily.

As I climbed back up the hill I was heaving mental sighs of relief that I'd escaped unscathed from the clutches of such a hideous girl, but at the same time I was kicking myself because I'd handled it so badly. By the time I'd reached the house I'd almost forgotten her. I was so out of breath from the climb I was glad to stagger into the house and flop into a chair. Sitting around the house for so long during the snow I'd obviously got out of condition and my ankle was aching again.

As I sat there I pulled the knot on the twine and unrolled the newspapers. They were old ones that Moses used as tablecloths and so on. Although the news was out of date it was quite fun reading about what was going on in the world, especially as, out here, none of it really touched me. Then I picked up the next to the last one and nearly fell out of the chair. Bang in the middle of the front page was a picture of me, looking like an acned Chinese! Underneath there was an article too. I'd often heard people complain about the press and now I knew exactly what they meant. For a start I resented being blazed across the front page (even if I did feel a small glow of pride as well), secondly, there was nothing in the article that wasn't true but it just didn't sound as if it was really me; and, thirdly, although it was quite neat to have complete strangers reading all about me I hated the idea of people I knew seeing it.

I read it casually, about six times, and then cut it out and hid it in a safe place. I was relieved I'd gone through the papers before Moses did. I could just see the expression on *his* face if he'd suddenly realised he was eating his supper off mine! I still felt the less he knew about me the safer I was.

'Why didn't you ever marry, Moses?' I asked that night after we'd eaten. My first proper meal had received grudging praise, and we were sitting in front of a roaring log fire. I don't know why I'd suddenly thought of that; in spite of myself my mind must still have been dwelling on the girl at the farm.

'No time, no money, no chance.'

'Come on, I bet you had lots of chances.'

'There was a girl in the village once,' his voice had gone unusually soft at the thought of her.

'What happened?' I asked quietly so as not to break the mood.

'We walked out a few times. It wasn't like it is today.'

'Didn't you want to get married?'

'Yes, I did. But there was Mam to think of. She'd worked herself to a standstill looking after us when Dad died. Even though we had the house we'd only what I earned coming in and there's many a time we had next to nothing in the house to eat. When I met this girl Mam was getting on and she wouldn't have been able to manage on her own up here.'

'If you'd married she'd have had help.'

'That's what I told her, but she wouldn't listen.'

'But it was your life. You let your mother rule your life?'

'She'd done a lot for me, I couldn't cross her.'

'What did your girl say about that?'

'It was all six of one and half a dozen of the other. I couldn't leave Mam on her own, and the girl wouldn't come and live up here with Mam, even if Mam would have let her.'

'So, what happened?'

'She married the coal man.'

I smiled to myself but it was clear Moses didn't think it was funny and I could see I had stirred a deep memory for him. As he looked at the dancing flames of the fire he seemed to be contemplating life as it might have been. It made me even more determined to do what I wanted instead of regretting things for the rest of my life. If only I really *knew* what I wanted to do.

'Have you got a girl-friend?' the old man broke the silence. It was his turn to smile now. 'I hear tell all you young fellows are wed by the time you leave school these days.'

'I go out with a few,' I felt myself blushing as I lied. 'Nothing steady though.'

'You're just like young Susan down at the farm. All the young men she's turned down, if you believe it her way.'

'Susan Bailey? I wouldn't have thought she got many offers.'

Moses looked me in the eye. 'When have you seen Susan Bailey?'

'When I went to get the milk. She looked as if she'd fallen in the midden.'

'Oh, yes?'

'And those huge glasses! I think girls look terrible in glasses.'

'I notice you took in the details!'

'I was waiting for the milk.'

'Oh, yes,' he said again and looked away at the fire. 'Well, you

51

want to watch yourself near that young lass. Charlie's got big ideas for her.'

'I haven't got any ideas for her at all, so he's welcome and anyone else. What about a game of cards?' I suggested trying to change the subject.

'Too late,' Moses said knocking his pipe out. 'I've got to be up early tomorrow.'

'Do you have to be up at the crack of dawn?'

'Like to make an early start.'

'What do you do down there?'

'Bit of mucking out, bit of fencing or hedging, anything Charlie needs a hand with. There isn't enough work for a farm-hand down there with all these machines but he often as not needs a bit of help. It suits me. He gives me an ounce of baccy from time to time or some feed for the chickens.'

'You mean he doesn't pay you?'

'I don't need the money, I'd rather have the goods.'

'If he wants you he ought to pay you. It sounds more like charity to me.'

'I don't take charity from anyone,' he shouted at me thumping the wooden arm of his chair.

'I take it from you. I don't pay for my bed and board.'

'No, but you're working for it. You look after the house and cook the meals. That's the price I charge you and you'll pay it.'

'But you still don't have to leave the house before it's light. Any time would do.'

'Not for me it wouldn't. Charlie's fair by me and I'm fair by him. You're right, maybe he doesn't need me all the time but when he does I'm there ready. They've been very good to me the Baileys. The day I go sauntering down there at midday I'll be in my box and that's an end of it.'

With that he slammed the door and clomped off up the stairs to bed without even saying good-night. It was clear I'd upset Moses by suggesting that Charlie only kept him on so that he could give him things but in a way it also showed the difference between Moses and my Dad.

Dad was always ready for a hand-out and if he'd found

somebody as kind as Charlie Bailey he'd have taken him for everything he could. But then Charlie would probably have sussed him out straight away and, even if he didn't, what Dad never realised was that every time he took a hand-out he was selling a bit more of himself, making himself a smaller man.

Moses was his own man. He didn't want a bungalow, home helps and Meals on Wheels, he just wanted his own life.

Chapter 7

*T*HE following day was what Moses called 'a bonus day'. The kind of weather that no reasonable human being has a right to expect at that time of year. The sky cleared early to a deep blue and even the birds seemed to be fooled into believing that Spring had arrived, judging by the chatter they set up.

After Moses left I set about my chores. When I'd finished it was so warm I took my coffee and some biscuits out to an old weather-worn seat which faced south, caught the warmth of the sun, and yet was sheltered from the breeze.

This was the life! I sat on the seat, arms akimbo, legs stretched out, eyes half closed, soaking the warmth of the sun. I was glad the subject of last night's discussion had not been raised again at breakfast. At least it showed Moses didn't bear grudges.

'Caught you!' The voice cut sharply through my drowsy thoughts. I'd always dreaded somebody creeping up on me, and now it had happened. 'Slacking!'

A girl was standing on the path. In a way she was a stranger and yet I thought I recognised her. Gone was the oversize jacket and funny hat but, most important of all, gone was all the muck. Instead she stood there, her blonde hair gleaming as it fell over the shoulders of her dark blue sweater, in a fashionably cut pair of grey cords and I could see she certainly hadn't got a figure like a barn! Susan Bailey. Only the glasses spoilt the effect.

'Sorry if I made you jump. I don't always look like a cowman.' I thought she was blushing slightly but she was also giving me a fairly steely glint with her blue, horn-rimmed, eyes.

'Sorry. You did give me a bit of a shock.'

'You didn't come down for the milk and I fancied a walk so I thought I'd bring it up.' She put the milk can down on the seat beside me. 'So, this is how you slave away all day?'

'Would you like a coffee?'

'Yes, please.'

She sat down on the seat and tilted her face up to get the full benefit of the sun. It caught her glasses and flashed into my eyes which brought me to my senses and I went in to get her drink.

I shivered once indoors. Whether that was a reaction after the heat of the sun or to the fact that she was waiting for me to go back I don't know. When she looked like a parcel tied in the middle I hadn't made a very good impression, but then I hadn't cared what she thought of me, now it seemed different.

As I stumbled back up the path, spilling coffee into the saucer, I knew I wanted her to stay but I didn't know how to get her to. She took the coffee without a word, carefully wiped the cup on the saucer to avoid dripping on her what I'd spilt, which made me feel terrific, sipped the coffee and pulled an awful face.

'You've put sugar in it!'

'Sorry, I didn't think.' Typical of me, I couldn't even get a simple thing like that right. 'I'll make you another.'

'I'll do it. I know my way around Moses' kitchen – I've been coming up here since I was knee high to a duck.'

While she was gone I picked up my own coffee. It was cold with a yukky skin like an eiderdown. The morning was going sour on me because of my usual ineptitude.

'You've made quite a difference in there,' she offered when she came back. 'There's only two layers of dust instead of three.'

While she sipped her coffee and I tried to ignore mine, which was beginning to turn my stomach now, the awful silence that seemed to always hang around us returned, and I couldn't think of anything interesting to say to break it.

'Dad's out mending fences with Moses.'

'Oh, yes?' I tried just to sound conversational but I was so

55

desperate it came out as if it was the most interesting piece of information I'd heard since Darwin's Theory on Evolution.

'Some cows got into the kale.'

I nodded, the conversation flagged again and my head was beginning to ache with the effort.

'Don't you think you ought to put the milk out of the sun?'

I muttered something about forgetting it, picked it up, fell over my feet as usual, and took it into the house. By the time I got back I was horrified to see that she'd finished her coffee and was standing up ready to go.

'I'd better be getting back. They'll wonder where I am.'

'Oh,' I said, with terrific panache. 'I wondered if we . . . .'

'What?' she tossed her hair back over her shoulder and waited.

'Er . . . I thought of taking a walk myself.'

'Good for you.'

Just like a girl. She knew what I wanted to say but she was enjoying watching me wriggle and squirm too much to help me out.

'Have you really *got* to go back?' I said in desperation.

'I have got jobs to do.'

'So have I, but mine can wait.'

'Where were you going for this walk of yours?' she looked at me as if she obviously didn't believe I really had been going anywhere. I shrugged. 'Have you been up to the wood yet?' I shook my head. 'Come on then, but I really mustn't be gone long.'

Going out of the gate on to the sandy track gave me the same scary feeling I'd had the day before of being off my territory. The idea of walking in the wood had occurred to me before but I didn't want to risk going alone. Moses reckoned he got enough walking done during his working day without wandering around for the sake of it. If I had gone alone I'd probably have got lost and then I would have had to ask somebody the way and I couldn't risk talking to strangers in case they recognised me and reported seeing me to the police.

Susan led the way through a wicket gate into the cool, green air of the conifers. As I entered the wood the feeling of being on foreign, unfamiliar ground grew so strong that I almost asked if we could go back, but I knew she'd think I was being silly so I gritted my teeth and we went on deeper into the wood.

I'd only ever had that feeling so strongly once before, when I'd come out of hospital. I'd only been in about a week, having my tonsils out, but I was in there long enough to have grown so familiar with my surroundings, and so protected from the outside, that when I first got out everything seemed big and unfamiliar. I suppose it was the same now with hiding away in Moses' house for so long.

It was all like one of those French films they show on BBC 2. Here was I, walking down an avenue of tall pines, with a girl. All I really needed now was for someone to write the dialogue.

'I suppose you know that you were all over the newspapers and the television?' she said suddenly without taking her eyes off the track ahead.

'Yes,' I nodded.

'I've never met anybody famous before,' she added and then laughed to herself.

'I suppose your Dad told you I was staying with Moses?'

'Yes, but I recognised you straight away even though it was a pretty dreadful photograph.'

'Yes, they were taken before I had my head transplant. The photographs are why I'm still here really. I got delayed by the blizzard,' I'd decided to miss out the bit about panicking and spraining my ankle, I still had some pride left. 'Then Moses got ill, I heard on the radio that everyone was out looking for me and I decided to stay on for a while.'

'Your Mum and Dad were upset about you.'

'I'll bet. Dad especially. I bet he's been crying into every sympathetic pint he's been bought.'

'Your Mum was very upset, she thought you'd died in the blizzard. They were out looking for you for days, you know.'

'Didn't look far, did they? – I'm only seventeen miles from

home now!' Susan turned and gave me a withering look. 'I'll get Moses to post a card for me as soon as he goes into the village.'

She relaxed a little after that and we walked on for a few yards in silence, breathing in the cool air which drifted out from the shadow of the trees. Sun shone on the path but it was dark and quiet between the close packed trunks of the firs, silently supporting their evergreen canopy. On another track I heard the galloping hooves of horses and through a gap in the undergrowth we caught a brief glimpse of the riders' colourful clothing as they swept past, then the quiet returned.

'Why did you run away?' she broke the silence at last. 'They said on television it was because you couldn't get a job.'

'That was part of it.'

'But lots of people don't get jobs as soon as they leave school, they don't all run away from home. Otherwise the hills would be alive with them.'

In one way I wished she hadn't brought this up because there was no knowing if she'd understand my reasons and at this stage I was quite keen on impressing her more than I had so far. On the other hand, I'd never discussed it with anybody before and it was time I did. I decided to risk it.

'When you get right down to it, I'm here because of my Dad. He made me leave school in the first place.'

'Made you?'

'My Dad is something else! He's out for anything he can get for nothing. He's never done an honest day's work in his life. He spends most of his time on the dole. A real no-hoper.'

'And your Mum?'

'She does her best. Dad found her a job, he's good at that sort of thing. The only thing is because it would affect Dad's Social Security payments nobody's supposed to know. The people Mum works for know about this, so she gets less than the going rate and works all the hours God sends.'

'She must get pretty fed up too.'

'She does. She spends about half her earnings in the Bingo Hall. I don't know whether that's because she wants to get away from Dad or if she expects to win a lot of money.'

'So your Dad wanted you to leave school and get a job like your mother?'

'No, he didn't even mind if it was legal and above board, as long as I got one. I think he's frightened his luck might not hold out and one day they might stop his payments. He just thought there ought to be somebody bringing in enough money for his beer and cigarettes.'

'Didn't you want to leave school?'

'I'd never even thought about it. I'd got quite decent O level results and I'd just assumed I was going back to school in the autumn to get my A levels.'

'What happened?'

'I told Dad about my results. When my friends told their parents they all got watches and bikes and things. All I got was my marching orders.'

'Hadn't he ever said anything before about leaving?'

'He'd never taken the slightest interest in what I did at school, so long as I went and the schools inspector didn't come snooping round asking awkward questions. Neither of them ever went to Open Nights or Parents Days or anything. My teachers thought I was an orphan!'

'What did they say at school when you told them you were leaving?'

'The Head said I was throwing away my chances. "Short term gains for long term losses", he called it. You see, he thought leaving was my idea.'

'Did you tell him it wasn't?'

'No point.'

'But your Headmaster could have talked to your father.'

'It wouldn't have made any difference. Dad had made his mind up and we'd already had one row about that. If I'd set the Headmaster on him there'd have been full-scale warfare and Mum always gets the worst of that.'

We heard the sound of the riders returning on their horses and, without a word, turned off down a steep, narrow track which was too overgrown with saplings for the horses to pass.

Out here only this feeling of being pursued stopped my problems seeming so far away as to be unreal.

'What happened when you started to look for a job?'

'I wrote letters, sometimes I even got answers, but not often. I went down to the Careers Advisory Office almost every day. Sometimes they'd send me for things but I was always just too late. Then I got two or three interviews, but they didn't lead anywhere. I'd either not got enough qualifications, or too many, or not the right kind, there was always a reason, but never a job. Dad swore I wasn't trying, but I was. I was only too glad to get out of the house.'

'What sort of jobs did you try for?'

'Everything from washer-up to steeplejack's hammer holder.'

'Was that what you wanted?' she sounded faintly surprised.

'I wanted anything!' I kicked a stone angrily out of the path. Then I calmed down again. 'Truth is I didn't know what I wanted. Remember, I wasn't even expecting to leave school, I thought I had another couple of years at least to decide what I wanted to do. With Dad on my back I just tried anything I might get, but there were a few thousand others in the same boat as me all after the same jobs.'

'So, you just gave up trying and ran away?'

'No!' I stopped and pulled her round to face me. 'Don't you see? If I'd gone on like that I knew I was just going to end up exactly like my Dad – another no-hoper. I'll never forget the first day he took me down to sign on. He had to go with me to keep an eye on any money that was going. Do you know, he was actually proud of me that day? Almost as if he was introducing me to his club. He introduced me to all his pals. He needn't have bothered. I'd seen them all before, hanging around waiting for the betting shop to open. Oh, there were other people there as well, some down on their luck through no fault of their own, they'd probably get jobs in the end, but not Dad's pals. For them this was their way of life, but not for me!'

I realised that I'd been shouting the last words into Susan's face. They echoed through the trees and died gently away. She pulled a wry face and turned to walk on but I stopped her again.

'I realised that if I didn't get away and run my own life,' I said very quietly but firmly so that she would get the point, 'that I might never have another chance. Dad had made a decision for me and it hadn't worked out. I wanted any more mistakes to be of *my* making, not his.'

Heated from our walk our breath was puffing out in clouds of steam ahead of us. Down on the road a car hooted noisily. We startled two wood-pigeons who executed a swift, perfectly symmetrical climb, swooping upwards in U-shaped arcs like Red Arrows on display then, seeing we meant them no harm, they flapped lazily out of sight.

'What are you going to do?'

'Originally I was going to Manchester to get a job.'

'If you couldn't get a job at home why would it be any easier there?'

'Bigger place, more chances.'

'And more people to take them.'

'I suppose.'

'But even if you got a job in Manchester, it's only going to be the same sort of job. How will that change anything?'

'I could go to evening classes and get my A levels. Then when I've made up my mind what I really want to do, I can do it, without anybody interfering.'

'Do you really think it'll be that easy? A job all day, study at night and don't forget you'll have to earn enough to keep yourself.'

'Nothing's that easy, but I've got to try.'

'But if you got a job you'd have to produce cards and then they'd trace you.'

'My Mum never handed over any cards. There are always people who'll take you on on the quiet.'

'Then you won't earn enough money, just like your mother.'

'Do you think I haven't thought of all that?' I was beginning to get angry again. I always do when I'm uncertain of my ground. 'It was a choice though and I've made it now!'

She thought very carefully before she spoke again. 'Are you sure it wouldn't be better to go home and have another try with your Dad?'

'After everything that's happened? My Dad, on average, is a right weed. But you don't cross him and get away with it. Once he's made his mind up TNT wouldn't shift it. At our house, when rows break out, you need a fall-out shelter and asbestos trousers.'

'I suppose it never occurred to you,' she said with a faint smile, 'that you're just like your Dad?'

'You mean I'm a weed?'

'No, obstinate! Pig-headed!'

'Look, if I go back now everything would just be ten times worse than it was before. I've got to prove that I'm right. Then I'll go back.'

'Dad recognised you straight away. Other people will too.'

'That's why I'm staying until people have forgotten me. But I still don't really understand why your father didn't go straight to the police as soon as he saw me.'

'Because it isn't any of our business. Dad was worried at first that you might have some sort of hold over Moses . . . .'

'Like a gun in my pocket?' I had to laugh at the idea and so did she.

'As soon as Moses said everything was all right that was the end of it. He told Mum and me, but if we told anyone he'd bang our heads against the barn door.'

'So, for now I'm safe.'

'Until the good weather comes. Hundreds of people come for walks up here. And then there's the riding school.'

'I'll probably be gone by then,' I said confidently and I was quite surprised that she went quiet after that. No more questions, we just walked.

It was only then that I really realised that I'd actually been talking to a real girl, sensibly. Maybe she didn't agree with everything that I'd said but at least she'd listened.

'Are you still at school?' I asked. It would be just my luck to discover she was about ten years older than I thought she was.

'Yes, I take my A levels in a year's time.'

'Why aren't you at school today then?'

'Because it's Sunday!'

'I should have thought of that! I haven't a clue what day of the week it is out here and it doesn't really seem to matter. I suppose it can get pretty boring if you live out here. What do you do all the time?'

'Suck straw and make rush baskets! What do you think we do out here? – We aren't a different race. We've got cars and electricity . . . . You people who live in cities make me sick, you think civilisation ends a hundred yards from your back door!'

I grinned. Living with Moses had distorted my view of country life. Of course not everybody relied on oil lamps and drew water from a well. While I was thinking about that she very quickly changed the subject.

'Did you tell your girl-friend you were going to run away?'

'No. I mean I haven't got one,' I had said it before I could stop myself. I didn't want her to know there was no competition. 'Nobody steady, anyway. Have you? Got a regular boy-friend?'

'Nobody special,' she said coolly, always one step ahead of me. Then, just to put me firmly in my place, she added, 'I never seem to meet the right sort of boy.'

Smarting from being so casually pushed out of the running I decided to hit back.

'Perhaps those goggles put them off.'

Without a word she turned and began to run up the track. I started off after her but she knew all the twists and turns so that, before very long, although I could hear her distant footsteps I knew there was no chance of catching her up.

I kicked myself for being so stupid. I hadn't meant to upset her all that much, I hadn't realised that she was so sensitive about her glasses. Compared to me she seemed so calm and self-assured.

Not knowing the wood it took me ages to find my way back to the cottage.

I hadn't noticed until Susan had left that the cloud had gathered across the sun and the wood now suddenly felt cold and eerie. Again I got the feeling of being exposed on the track and when I heard a group of horse riders coming towards me I decided to push my way through the close packed lower branches of the trees.

Their branches scratched my face and caught at my clothes leaving powdery smears of green on my arms and legs. It took me ages to reach another path and I was so relieved to be back in the open that I decided to stick to it and risk being spotted.

I must have walked for half an hour without seeing anything I recognised. To me one tree was just like another. If I'd suddenly found myself in a strange part of the city it wouldn't have bothered me. I would simply have kept on walking until I came to somewhere that I knew, but out here I felt very lost and began to wonder if I ever really would get out.

Just then through a gap in the trees I saw that I had managed to walk to the edge of the wood. I climbed over the fence into a field and felt much better now that I was in open country. I followed the fence round. At last it brought me to the well and the path for home.

That night my legs still ached from the unaccustomed exercise and I felt rough about Susan's hasty departure. Even Moses noticed how quiet I was.

'Did you have a row with young Susan?'

'What do you mean?'

'Charlie and me were working in the bottom meadow and we saw you going off towards the wood. You don't seem full of the joys of spring now, so I suppose you had a row?'

'Something like that.' I couldn't see what business it was of his anyhow.

'I warned you about Susan. Charlie Bailey's got big plans for her. He wants her to marry a farmer's son. You shouldn't go getting any ideas into your head about her.'

'I suppose they've got everything all mapped out. Just like my Dad and just like your mother. She stopped you getting married didn't she? – Well, I'm going to do what I want and nobody's going to interfere.'

He didn't say anything else but I could see that I'd managed to put my foot in it twice on the same day.

Chapter 8

*A*FTER my outburst Moses was fairly quiet for a couple of days and I knew there was no chance of making it up with Susan who was back at school for the week. Apart from keeping an eye on the lane to see if I could catch a glimpse of her there was nothing I could do and time seemed to drag along.

One night Moses came puffing across the yard with a huge feather mattress on his back. He looked like one of those burglars you see in comics carrying a bag marked 'SWAG'.

He threw it down on the kitchen floor and sank breathless into a chair.

'Your bed,' he jerked a thumb at it. 'Mrs Bailey sent it up for you. Can't have you sleeping on that old sofa for ever.'

He helped me to get it up the stairs and when we'd spread the feathers out, so that it was a thin oblong again, it was quite comfortable.

'Take up anything else you want,' he said.

I spent the whole of the next day cleaning out the room and collecting spare furniture from the front parlour. The room I'd chosen was the front bedroom which got the morning sun and looked down across the valley. Through a small side window I could also look out towards the wood.

By the time I'd added a chair and a table, even though there was no base for the mattress and it had to lie on the bare floorboards, it felt quite homely, almost as if it was mine.

When I'd finished it all I lay down on the bed and through the windows all I could see was sky. It was almost like being at sea watching the clouds scudding by. I had taken down the damp stained curtains. Out here I didn't mind being woken up by the sun each morning. It was an odd contrast to my little box of a room at home which only looked out at the stalks of the other high rise blocks around us. If I hadn't got on the wrong side of Susan everything would have been perfect.

That night, as we sat in our accustomed places on opposite sides of the fireplace (I think the world would have ended if we'd ever changed sides) reading the old newspapers that had come up from the farm, I glanced up and watched Moses peering in the poor light at the newspaper. He had no glasses but used a carved, ivory-handled magnifying glass the lens of which was secured by a band of brass. It looked like a small table-tennis bat.

He never spent long reading the paper and if I asked him if he'd read a particular story he never had.

Earlier that evening we'd had baked beans with our meal and I remembered asking him to open the tin. At the time I didn't really think about it, but he couldn't find the tin, although it was on the shelf in the dresser right in front of him. It wasn't the usual brand with a picture of the beans on the label but it had the words 'BAKED BEANS' printed large enough. When I picked up the tin from under his nose he'd just made a joke of it and I'd forgotten until now.

As I watched him I realised he wasn't reading the paper at all, just looking at the pictures. Suddenly I began to wonder if he could read. Reading's taken for granted these days, almost everybody can read, but it must have been sixty years since Moses went to school and perhaps things were different then.

The problem was I didn't know how to approach the subject. I felt that it might injure his pride, and yet he'd managed without being able to read for all these years so perhaps it didn't bother him too much. In the end I decided to take the direct approach.

'Would you like me to read bits out to you?'

'Umm?' he looked up and I thought for a moment he was

going to be angry with me but he just quietly set the magnifying glass down and passed me the paper. 'Aye, all right. It hurts my eyes in this poor light.'

I didn't press him any further. I had given him a chance to admit it if he wanted to but he hadn't taken it. I read out a few of the items which I thought might interest him and stopped when I thought he'd had enough.

'I suppose we ought to get a new battery for that wireless,' he said after a pause. 'I hear young people don't like being without their ears stuck to one of them things.'

'It would be nice to keep up with what's going on in the world,' I said. I wasn't going to get drawn into some argument about the merits of pop music and I was pretty sure that my name wasn't likely to be mentioned in the news again now that the snow had gone. 'You get a battery when you go down to the shop and I'll have a fiddle to see if I can get it going.'

He stretched his arms and then knocked his pipe out on the side of the grate before slipping it straight into his bib pocket as usual.

'You'll set yourself on fire, one day, doing that,' I said.

'I'd not be missed,' he said without a trace of emotion.

'I'd miss you,' I grinned.

'Aye, maybe,' he muttered and went off up to bed.

I collected my candle and, for the first time, followed the old man up the stairs to sleep in my own room. Having been used to undressing in front of the fire until now I was shivering by the time I got between the sheets. How the old man managed was a mystery to me.

Maybe it was because of the unfamiliar bed, despite its being more comfortable than the old sofa with the spring which had always managed to stick into me wherever I lay, but that night it was a while before I fell asleep. I lay there wondering how I could tackle Moses about his reading, at one point I even wondered if I could teach him, and my mind also kept drifting on to Susan and whether I would get the chance to apologise.

Next morning the sun shining in my eyes woke me. There had been a slight frost and I threw my clothes on as quickly as I could and got downstairs to the warmth of the kitchen fire. Having my own room was a mixed blessing!

'I'm going to start digging,' he announced over breakfast.

'I'll help,' I offered.

He gave me an odd sort of look. 'Have you done any digging before?'

'I don't think so. I don't remember, but I'm sure I can learn,' I said, thinking he must be mad. After all what is there to putting your spade in the earth, lifting it up and turning it over?

'Just as you like,' he said. 'You finish up in here first and I'll make a start.'

By the time I'd done the dishes and collected the water he had about an hour's start on me but he hadn't done that much and seemed to be moving very slowly and deliberately. The work was obviously heavy for a man of his age. I grabbed a spade and set to with a will.

I was the first to rest. My furious burst of energy was soon spent but as I leant on my spade and mopped my brow Moses was still going.

Not wanting to be shamed by a man three times my age I set off again but very quickly a pain developed in the small of my back and sweat was running in a salty stream out of my hair and into my eyes. With difficulty I straightened up and tugged my jersey off but the breeze quickly chilled the sweat on my back so I put it back on again. Moses was still going, his speed unchanged from when he'd started.

'No need to rush,' he looked up and grinned at me. 'You can give up and have a rest if you like.'

'I'm all right,' I said, through gritted teeth. I was determined not to be beaten.

When we stopped for lunch of bread and cheese I was very relieved, but Moses looked as fresh as a daisy. Whatever position I got my back in against the wooden chair it seemed to ache.

Moses grinned at me. 'You go at it like a bull at a gate. What doesn't get done will keep for later. When you start something new, find your pace, then stick to it.'

Although it was better in the afternoon I had to admit I'd had enough by three and I was grateful when Moses suggested I should clean my tools off and go and collect the milk. As I rubbed the spade with an oily rag to keep it from rusting, I watched him still using the pace I'd scorned earlier in the day and admired the fact that he'd covered at least four times the amount of ground.

'I thought because I was younger I'd do better.'

'You will with more practice. I've got seventy-five years' experience to match against your youth.'

At first the walk down the lane loosened up my knotted muscles but by the time I reached the farm I was beginning to wonder how I'd feel on the journey back up the hill.

I was about to knock on the door, half hoping I might see Susan, when Charlie Bailey loomed up around the end of the building.

'Come for the milk? Give me your can, you wait here.'

As I waited in the yard I thought I saw one of the curtains stir at an upstairs window but I decided it must be my imagination. By now I'd almost convinced myself that I couldn't really be bothered with anyone as touchy as she was, but not quite.

'If you're looking for Susan, she's out.'

'I wasn't,' I lied.

He picked up the roll of newspapers in his great hand and made it look like a spill. Perhaps Moses was right, I should try to keep on the right side of Charlie Bailey! He handed me the milk can and we were left standing awkwardly with each other, neither knew quite what to say.

'Moses decided to make a start on the garden today,' I offered.

'Aye, he said he might.'

'He said he'd be down again on Thursday unless you need him.'

'Aye,' Mr Bailey just nodded; the expression on his face gave little away but it was clear he'd be glad when I'd gone.

'I've been helping him,' I added hoping to improve his impression of me as a no good runaway who was living like a parasite on Moses.

'Have you?' he looked scornful. 'Then you'd better get back

up there while you can still walk. I don't suppose you're used to hard work! You might need a day in bed tomorrow.'

With that he turned on his heel and left me to slink out of the yard, defeated.

By the time I got back to the cottage I began to realise that what he'd said was true. All I wanted was a good hot bath and my bed. A bath was out of the question. It meant collecting extra buckets of water and filling the huge copper and then pouring the contents into the tin bath which hung on a nail in the yard. The fact that a dead pig had been one of the copper's most recent occupants was enough to put me off, even ignoring the physical effort involved.

Instead, after our meal I collapsed, painfully, into a chair and examined the blisters that had formed on the palms of both hands as I nodded off to sleep in the heat from the fire.

'Nothing like working in the open to make you feel tired if you're not used to it,' Moses said with quiet glee.

I'd had enough country homilies for one day so I wished him good-night and climbed the stairs to bed. I wasn't so keen on my makeshift mattress as I had been the previous night. For one thing I wasn't sure if I could get down to floor level and for another if I got down I wasn't at all certain that I'd be able to get up again the following day. For the first time since I'd left home I almost wished that I was getting into my own old bed, but there was no doubt that once in bed I didn't have the difficulties I'd had the previous night in getting to sleep.

Chapter 9

WHEN I woke up I was relieved to see rain pouring down the windows and when I creaked out of bed a heavy mist concealed the valley. At least there would be no more digging today!

Moses had got up early and made the same discovery, so that by the time I eventually got downstairs the kitchen was like a sauna, with condensation pouring down the windows and walls. He had decided to have a baking day.

The contrast between my bedroom and the kitchen soon had me shedding pullovers. Great tongues of flame leapt up the chimney as Moses stoked up to get the old-fashioned oven to the required temperature.

As I perched on a corner of the table eating my breakfast Moses plunged his arms into mounds of dough for bread and then set about making a ton of pastry.

'Don't bake often – it's too much trouble heating the oven,' he gasped, as he pounded the dough with blows that made the table legs protest. 'So when I do I make sure it's worth while.'

As bread rose under damp cloths he put his first pies into the oven and then they in turn were quickly replaced by pasties and eventually, around lunch-time, by the loaves themselves.

The hot pies straight from the oven smelt delicious and we ate an apple one for lunch with some custard. He'd used slices of dried apple which hung on a string that stretched from one corner of the picture rail to the other. They were dusty, shrivelled and brown before they went into the pie, but I had to admit that the pie was a terrific success and the old man obviously knew what he was doing.

As soon as we'd washed up I opened the door for some air and discovered the rain had eased off.

'Shall I go and get the milk while the rain's stopped?' I asked. Any excuse to escape this Turkish Bath was good enough for me.

Moses looked up and nodded. His arms, overalls and hair were thick with flour but he was obviously enjoying himself without any help from me.

After the heat of the kitchen the damp mist which swept across the valley and dampened my face and hair was very refreshing, and I chuckled at the thought of Moses stuck up there in his fusty kitchen. Moses was always on the go while there was daylight about. There's something about old people, they either never stir from the best seat in the house or, like Moses, they're never still.

For me time is just a measure to the next thing. The next meal, the next day at school or the next programme on the telly. Older people seem to use time differently.

Moses measured time by daylight. Not having electricity he got all his jobs done in the best light and then sat and chatted when the light faded and he had to light the lamp.

When I got to the farm I'd half expected to see Susan hanging around the buildings, she was still very much on my mind; but a can of milk and the newspapers were waiting for me in the porch so I didn't even have an excuse to knock on the door.

The yard was absolutely silent and still, just as it had been the first time I went down there. The rain glistened on the concrete and not even a dog stirred. Disappointed, I turned for home.

I'd just reached the end of the buildings, and was about to turn up our track, when I heard a voice.

'Hi!'

I stopped in my tracks and was about to turn round; I knew the voice was Susan's.

'Don't turn round, just keep walking slowly. I'll meet you up by the gate into the wood, I'll go across the fields.'

73

I left the can of milk at the cottage gate and hared up to the wood in case she'd got bored with waiting and gone home. When I first arrived there was no sign of her and I thought she must have changed her mind.

'Come through the gate you clown, everyone can see you there!' she whispered fiercely from the other side of the wall.

I pushed open the gate and found her squatting on a log with her back against the rough stone wall. I plumped down beside her and we fell into one of our well known uncomfortable silences.

'Moses is baking.'

'He makes good bread but half the pies go off before he gets the chance to eat them. Watch out for the mouldy ones or you'll die of food poisoning.'

'He said you're going to marry a farmer's son,' I said firmly avoiding her eyes.

'Who did?'

'Moses. He said your father had got it all worked out.'

'He thinks he has,' she leapt to her feet and for a moment I thought she was going to take off again in a huff. 'Come on let's walk. Nobody will see us in the wood on a day like this.'

We squelched along the track. The sand we'd walked along before had turned to muddy puddles with the heavy rain and the branches of the trees were edged with droplets of water which dripped on us as the slightest breath of wind stirred them.

This time I kept my mouth firmly shut and waited for her to speak first.

'Dad wanted me to be a boy,' she said at last.

'He didn't make a very good job of it then,' I grinned but she didn't.

'He wanted someone to pass the farm on to when he retires. Mum can't have any more children so they're stuck with just me.'

'That's hard luck for them then isn't it?'

'No it isn't. It's hard luck for me. If I can't be a farmer I can be a farmer's wife so, when I leave school, he intends to pack me off to agricultural college. Partially so that I'll make a good farmer's wife but partially in the hope that I'll get so desperate for male company that I'll marry one of the students.'

'Is that what you want?' I asked hoping I knew the answer.

'It certainly isn't.'

'I should hope not. You're far too good to waste on some great sweaty farmer.'

'Hang on a minute!' she stopped dead in her tracks. 'I think you've got a very distorted view of life in the country. We aren't all bumpkins you know and the farmer's sons round here don't go around with smocks on and straws hanging out of the corners of their mouths, wearing vacant expressions.'

'I'm sorry,' I mumbled. I'd done it again! 'I only thought . . . .'

'As a matter of fact,' she cut in, 'they're very nice boys and I know two who get their suits at Austin Reed and drive Aston Martins.'

'If you're that keen on them why don't you marry one of them then?' I retorted angrily. I was getting fed up with the whole business by now.

'One, because I don't think I'd make them a very good wife, because, two, I don't happen to be very interested in farming.' She started to stomp away down the track and I grinned to myself and followed.

'What do you want to do then?'

'Commercial Design.'

'Commercial Design?'

'Yes, in a pottery. Is there something wrong with that?'

'No,' I said trying to wipe the surprised look off my face. In the end though I couldn't help it, I had to ask. 'You mean, you *want* to work in a city?'

'Why on earth not? I go to school in one,' I was irritating her again. 'Why do you have to think in clichés?'

'I just thought being born in the country you'd prefer it out here.'

'Well, I don't. I mean I quite like living out here but I don't want to work here. I'm not Moses and this is the twentieth century, but just try telling Dad that. So, that's what all the fuss is about. That and the fact that Dad doesn't like the idea of me meeting a runaway hippy.'

'Me? A hippy?'

'To Dad anyone who isn't a farmer is either a hippy or a pansy, it's just his way. Either way, he doesn't want me to have anything to do with you. I suppose, also, he thinks that you might get into trouble with the police eventually and some of that might rub off on me. So, in a way, you could say I've got the same problem as you. I want one thing, he wants another.'

'What will you do about it?'

'I don't really know,' she sighed. 'I thought of failing my exams so that I can't get into Agricultural College but then I wouldn't be able to get into the Technical School to do what I want either! Cutting off my nose to spite my face. I don't know what I'll do in the end.'

'But you won't run away?' my voice sounded guilty as I asked the question.

'No, I won't. But it isn't really the same for me is it? By the way, have you written to your Mum yet, you said you would?'

'No, I haven't.'

'Oh, Peter! Promise me you will. She must be dreadfully upset.'

She looked at me so earnestly that I couldn't refuse. 'I'll write, I promise.'

'This week-end?'

'Yes, this week-end, don't nag. Letters reminds me, I was going to ask you about Moses. Can he read?'

'I don't know, why?'

'It suddenly occurred to me a couple of days back that he was looking at the paper but not really reading it and he's never had a letter delivered since I've been staying with him.'

She shook her head, 'The postman wouldn't go up there, he'd leave it with us, but I don't remember anything coming for him for years, unless Dad just hands them over and I don't see them.'

'The day after I got there I was fiddling with some books and two airmail letters dropped out. I'm sure they've never been read if he can't read them, and they could be important.'

'I don't see what you can do about it.'

'Well, I could read them to him, couldn't I? Maybe even write a reply for him. The only thing is he's so prickly I don't know how to approach him. It's just that he's been so kind to me I'd like to do something for him in return but I don't want to upset him.'

'Ask him,' she said in the end. 'I expect he'll be pleased. After all he seems to like you otherwise he'd have chucked you out on your ear ages ago. Moses doesn't suffer fools gladly.'

'I'm not sure, but I think that was almost a compliment,' I said with a grin.

'Take it any way you like,' she said coolly.

I decided it was time for my big apology and I took a deep breath before I risked it. 'I'm sorry about what I said about your glasses the other day. I didn't mean to upset you.'

She bit her bottom lip and went slightly red. 'No, it was stupid of me, I'm oversensitive about them. I don't have any choice. I'm very long-sighted. Without them I couldn't even read or walk about the place without falling over.'

'But do they have to have horn rims?'

'That's to put the farmers' sons off,' she grinned. 'Dad was furious when I brought them home. He threatened to smash them, until I told him how much they cost. They've worked so far anyway.'

'How do you mean?'

'Not a farmer's son in sight.'

'Just a minute,' I stopped and she stood opposite me. 'Did you mean what you said about walking about without them?'

'Yes,' she shrugged, 'blind as a bat.'

'Good,' I said, then I lifted them off her face and kissed her.

Chapter 10

While I finished the breakfast washing up I was busy
compiling a list of the girls I'd known who hadn't wanted to kiss
me. To the bottom of that list had to be added Sarah Williams,
who actually let me kiss her but then wiped her mouth with the
back of her hand.

I'd just decided that Susan had great taste in men when I heard
voices out in the yard. I bolted the back door and nipped
upstairs. By then the voices had moved through the yard and out
into the garden.

Moses' room was the only one with a good view of the garden
so I crept in and peered out from behind one of the curtains. I
still couldn't see anyone but through the glass I thought there
were three voices.

Two of them I recognised as Moses and Charlie Bailey but the
third one sounded rather high pitched and croaky. If it had been
my room I could have opened the window to hear better but
Moses was not a great believer in fresh air on the inside of the
house.

'Everything in it's proper place,' he'd said very firmly one day
when I suggested airing the house a bit. 'Fresh air is made for
outside, not inside!'

To emphasise his point he'd screwed the window to the frame
and packed round the cracks with newspaper! It was a bit like
his philosophy about baths which, according to him, washed
away your natural oils and weakened your skin!

I could clearly see the vast bulk of Charlie and the small,
dumpy figure of Moses but, although I could still hear the third

person, there was no sign of them until suddenly a pink, hairy piglet leapt out of Charlie's arms and made off across the garden with an ear-splitting squeal of freedom!

I ran down the stairs and out into the garden to watch as the two men lumbered clumsily around after the frightened animal. No sooner had they got it cornered at one end of the garden than it slipped between them with a squeal of triumph and made off for the other end.

Tears rolled down my face as I watched the men. Charlie was getting puffed and stopped to mop his face with his cap while Moses cornered the piglet for the umpteenth time only to realise that he was alone and couldn't hold it.

'Don't just stand there like a lemon!' shouted Moses. 'Help.'

'I'm sorry, but you ought to see yourselves!'

'Never mind that,' said Moses who was obviously in no mood for jokes. 'We're trying to drive him towards the sty.'

The door of the sty was propped open with a piece of wood. All three of us went into a half crouch, like rugby players waiting for the ball to come out of a scrum, and drove it slowly towards the open door. We'd almost got him in when a puff of wind blew against the door, shifted the wood that held it and the door slammed shut frightening the piglet almost out of its life. Again it slipped between us and ran off across the garden.

'Fix it properly this time,' said Charlie who's temper was getting strained. He pointed at the ground beside him. 'You stand next to me this time.'

To be honest I thought they had been making fools of themselves so far and I failed to see how one small piglet could possibly outwit two grown men.

Again we edged it back towards the sty. It would stop from time to time, drop its snout to admire some interesting garden smell and then slowly, inch by inch continue on its way issuing quite deep grunts for such a small animal. It looked so innocent and harmless that I began to feel quite sorry for it. The two men must have been scaring it out of its wits.

Then, just as we'd almost got it to the sty, it suddenly turned and charged straight at me.

'Stop him!' cried Moses.

'Head him off,' shouted Charlie.

I tried, I really did try. In what must have taken seconds, but seemed like an hour, I saw the inoffensive piglet turn into a rhinoceros then back into a piglet, and by that time it had shot through my legs and I was lying on my back while the two men took their turn for a good laugh.

'You ought to see your face,' Moses howled.

'Thought you knew better than us, did you?' Charlie managed to mutter between laughs that sounded like a fog-horn and echoed off the buildings.

I dusted myself off and they recovered themselves but then we discovered we'd lost sight of the piglet altogether.

'I didn't see it go,' said Moses.

'Well, it can't have vanished into thin air,' Charlie added and we all three set to searching the garden for the wretched creature. I was the one who found it.

'It's over here.'

'Where?' Moses looked perplexed. 'I can't see it.'

'In the sty!' I pointed at the pink animal, tired and bored with the excitement of the chase who was sniffing round the sack of meal Moses had brought up from the farm and dumped in a corner of the sty.

Thankfully Moses closed the door after it, bolted it firmly and we all three went back to the house for a cup of tea.

'That's another job for you,' Moses said as we sat round the table with steaming mugs in front of us. 'You can look after the pig. Only I'll show you how to do it. I don't want it fattened up as quickly as those hens.'

Charlie roared with laughter so loudly it set the glass shade of the oil lamp rattling and it was obvious they'd shared that joke before. I just sat there feeling awkward.

'Long job fattening a pig,' mused Charlie as his mirth subsided. 'Think you'll still be here in six months' time?'

'I might be,' I said quietly. I knew there was more behind his words than he was letting on yet.

'I wondered if you might be thinking of moving on soon?' he

80

said, sipping his tea noisily. 'I expect it's a lot of extra work for Moses, you being here.'

'No, it's not!' Moses snapped in his best mind-your-own-business voice.

'Only the other day you said he was eating you out of house and home,' Charlie looked at Moses daring him to deny it.

'I said no such thing,' Moses said firmly, much to my relief. 'I only said he's got a better appetite these days. He didn't eat more than a fly when he first got here, but now he polishes off a good plateful, don't you, boy?'

I nodded. The less I said at the moment the better.

'But he works for his keep, I see to that, don't you worry. There are no free rides here.'

'Mmmm!' Charlie said meaningfully and drained the last of his tea at a gulp. He pushed himself up and made his way towards the door.

'All I can say is, if you're thinking of hanging around here much longer, I'd rather you kept away from young Susan. She's got important exams coming up this summer and I don't want her mind wandering. You understand me?'

I nodded again, biting back what I really wanted to say to him.

'In fact Moses,' he added, 'I'd be glad if you'd bring the milk up yourself and then this young fellow will have no excuse for hanging about the farm.'

'Just as you like,' Moses said; he wasn't going to be drawn into this discussion and I couldn't blame him, it was my fight really.

'No offence, but I'd prefer her not to get mixed up with a townie!' he turned back towards Moses. 'Are you coming down now?'

'I'll have a bite to eat first.'

'Just as you like,' he nodded to Moses and then turned back to give me a severe look. 'Just you think on what I've said!'

With that he shut the door firmly and as I listened to the sound of his boots receding across the yard I gripped the table to try and control my anger. It was just as it always was with my father! Charlie Bailey had told me what I was to do and instead of standing up to him I'd just sat there and said nothing. I sat there feeling disgusted with myself and yet, at the same time, I knew no matter what I'd said it would have made no difference. It would probably have made matters worse, especially for Susan. But I still wished I hadn't just sat there like a stuffed dummy!

Moses began to hack two great lumps off one of the loaves he'd baked the previous day. He smeared them with butter, dropped them on to plates with wedges of cheese and pushed one across to me, but I didn't feel like eating.

'Don't take any notice, it's just his way,' Moses said as he bit a great lump out of the bread and crammed it into his mouth. 'But you can't say I didn't warn you!'

'It's none of his business. If Susan wants to see me he can't stop her.'

'Oh yes he can! Maybe he can't make her do all the things he wants her to, but he can stop her doing any he doesn't.'

'I suppose you're right,' I agreed reluctantly. 'I won't go near the farm, but if she comes up here I'm not going to send her away.'

'Don't forget, lad,' he said, shaking his head, 'you're in a poor position to make the rules, nor yet break them. If Charlie took it into his head to report you to the police he still can.'

'You said he wouldn't do that unless you said so.'

'That was when it was my business, your being here. Now it seems you're determined to make it his business. What affects Susan affects him. I couldn't stop him doing what he thought fit, could I?'

'I suppose not.'

'It comes down to what you want most, lad. You can stay here in safety, or you can risk seeing Susan and take the consequences.'

'Things haven't changed much have they?' I snapped, knowing that I was defeated.

'How d'you mean?'

'It's like the dark ages out here. It's just the same as when they stopped you going with your girl.'

'It's not the same at all.'

'Just my luck, isn't it? First chance I get of a real girl-friend and you all gang up on me.'

'Stop sounding like a spoilt child,' Moses scolded. 'It isn't a bit like that. The fact is, you don't belong round here.'

'All right, I'll pack up and go!' I stood up and sent my chair squealing viciously across the quarry tiles.

'I'd finish your bread and cheese first,' he said quietly without looking up from his own plate.

I plumped back down into the chair. I knew my outburst sounded pompous and empty. I had nowhere to go.

'I know how you feel,' he went on. 'But it's the truth and you might as well face up to it. You aren't going to stay around here for ever are you? – You can't. When things quieten down you'll have to move on for your own sake. One way or the other you'll have to leave Susan behind, so it might just as well be sooner than later. That way less damage will be done, to both of you.'

I let out a sigh of complete defeat, 'I suppose you're right.'

'I know I am. The more you see of each other the worse it'll be later when you part, but part you'll have to, mark my words!'

'But I couldn't send her away if she came up here,' I repeated. Moses shrugged. 'I couldn't!'

'Think about this then. I'm fond of Susan too, I've known her since the day she was born and I don't want to see her upset. I've not known you so long but you don't seem a bad sort of a chap. There's not much wrong with you that a clump round the ear wouldn't put right.' I grinned at him. 'But if you go on like this you'll have Charlie Bailey getting so mad he's bound to go down to the police. Then everyone'll get upset. You'll be in trouble and so will I.'

'Why you, you didn't ask me to come here?'

'No, but I didn't send you away either, did I? Charlie Bailey tells me they've had the police of four counties out looking for you. I don't suppose they'd be best pleased to know you'd been up here all that time.'

'But Charlie Bailey's known all this time. He'd get his share of the blame.'

'It isn't the same,' Moses said firmly. 'I don't want a lot of folks coming up here and poking their noses into my affairs.'

'I don't understand. It'd be no worse for you than for me.'

'Perhaps not, but there's a lot of folks who can't take their noses out once they've got them in. I like to keep myself to myself. People in the village understand that and they leave me be, but when outsiders come round, busybodies, there's no knowing where it might lead.'

'What sort of busybodies?'

'These social workers, or whatever they're called.'

'They could help you.'

'I don't want anybody's help,' Moses thumped his hand down on the table and made the plates jump. 'I can manage all right just the way I am, thank you.'

'But it could make life easier for you,' I said, trying to make it sound reasonable. I heard Dad talk about this sort of thing for years. 'There's improvement grants and all sorts of things I expect you're entitled to.'

'I call that charity and I won't have it!'

'But it's only like drawing your pension.'

'I don't draw no pension.'

'What?' I sat back open mouthed.

'What bit of money I need I work for. Always have, always will.'

'You mean you don't draw the old age pension?'

'I've seen what happens to people who go on the Poor. Once you draw that you can't call your soul your own. They're after you for this and then the other. While I've got this place and earn the money I need I don't owe nobody for nothing and I don't ask anybody for nothing.'

'But what'll happen when you can't look after yourself any more?' I said carefully. 'You are getting on, you know.'

'When I can't manage for myself then I'll be ready for me box. The money for that's in the blue vase on the mantel. Anyway, I'd be glad if you kept yourself to yourself and don't cause any more bother between you and Charlie. Understand?'

Chapter 11

'You're entitled,' my Dad had always said, 'that's what the Welfare State is for.'

There was a big gulf between his beliefs and Moses. Moses obstinately refused to accept anything he hadn't earned while my father would take the bottle out of a baby's mouth if he got the chance. Moses struggled along in a cold, mouldy cottage while my father lived in a council flat on hand-outs.

For the first few years of my life I'd been clothed entirely by the Salvation Army until they cottoned on and we took our custom to Oxfam and Jumble Sales. Entirely, that is, apart from socks and underwear. Mam said it wasn't decent wearing other people's underwear.

I was the first kid in our school to have patches on my jeans. Now, everyone does it but mine were practical, not decorative. They covered up real holes. Only when the patches were in danger of joining together did I get a fresh pair.

Somehow I couldn't get it across to Dad that Social Security was intended for people who couldn't help themselves, not for scroungers to simply help themselves. It was to help people like Moses who needed help, and here he was turning it down instead of grabbing it with both hands. Whilst I didn't believe in Dad's philosophy I couldn't understand Moses. Dad deep down believed he was doing everyone at the Social Security Office a favour with his regular visits.

'It's people like me that keep people like them in work,' he once told me proudly.

When Moses came back up from the farm that night he handed me a note.

'I told her, this is the last time I'm doing this,' he sounded really cross. 'I'm not going behind Charlie's back, even for Susan.'

I opened the note and gazed at her writing. Never having seen it before it quite surprised me, very neat italics written in jet black ink which stood out starkly from the piece of ring-file paper she'd used. It suited her, the writing, firm and clear. Hungrily I started to read the contents hoping that she had decided to stand up to her father even if I hadn't, but it wasn't a bit like that.

> 'Dear Peter,
>   Dad has told me everything he said to you. As usual we had a row but I don't want to spoil things for you. He said that he'd report you to the police if I saw you again so, in the end, I had to agree not to.
>   I'm sorry things have turned out like this because I was just getting to like you and I think you like me a bit too, in spite of my glasses.
>   If I ever get the chance to slip up to the cottage, while Dad is away somewhere, I will. But in case I don't see you again, I hope all goes well for you. Think of me sometimes, probably, knowing my luck, married to one of those great sweaty farmers you mentioned. (Not if I know it!)'

There was a bit more but it was fairly personal and rather what you'd expect a girl to write. I rather liked it though because no girl had ever written it to me before. Come to think of it, no girl had ever written anything to me before, unless you count Cousin Alice from Blubberhouses, and I don't. Dad always insists I send her a Christmas present because he knows Cousin Alice's Dad's got a bit of money and Dad reckons he might get his sticky fingers on some of it if I keep in with her. Every year Mum buys something and sends it in my name and every year Cousin Alice copies something out of a book on how to write thank-you letters and sends it to me. What a farce! This wasn't in the same league. I day-dreamed about it, and Susan, right through supper until in my head it had ceased to be prose and turned into pure poetry.

I was so pleased with Moses for bringing it up that I decided it was time to return the favours he'd done me. He was fumigating the place, as usual, with his old pipe and I got up and started innocently ferreting around the radio amongst the old books.

'That old copy of *Tom Sawyer* – have you seen it?'

'Upstairs in my room.'

'Can I get it? I've always meant to read it and I never have.'

He nodded and I bounded upstairs. I'd got over the first hurdle but as I came down, more slowly, I knew I had a much more difficult one to get over yet. My heart was thumping as I closed the stairs door and walked back over to my chair.

'I'd best have those letters out of it,' he stretched out a brown claw towards me.

I slipped the envelopes from between the pages. They'd been opened so perhaps I was barking up the wrong tree.

'Have you ever read them?' I asked at last, trying to sound casual but my voice sounded hoarse to me. The clock ticked away the seconds as I waited for his answer. He hadn't taken his eyes from the envelopes. I knew that if anything went wrong now I would never have the courage to approach the subject again.

'Not for a long time. Maybe you could read them over for me, my eyes are tired tonight.'

'Yes, of course.' I could hardly get the letters out of their envelopes quickly enough. They were postmarked Australia and one had been sent on January nineteen fifty-eight, the other in August.

As I slipped the January one out I noticed there were some coloured photographs but I put those aside for later. I wanted to get on with the letters, and the rest of my plan, before he changed his mind.

'Dear Moses,

I know you will be surprised to hear from me after all these years, but it's been on my mind a good while to write to you. I always feel guilty about running off and leaving you to look after Mum but I knew it was something I had to do, having seen what happened to you. You just got set in your ways, but I knew there was no future for farm-workers when the war ended. Machinery would soon see to that.

I knew that that place couldn't support two of us and as you already had your job fixed I thought I'd better be the one to go.

Things weren't easy out here at first. They said it was a land of opportunity but, just like everywhere else, you had to make your own opportunities. By the time I'd got here, of course, I was broke so I started at rock bottom.

I won't tell you now everything that's happened but believe me it hasn't been easy, and if I had known how hard it would be perhaps I'd never had left home in the first place.

Anyway, now I've got a place of my own, just a few hundred acres (which probably sounds a lot to you but it's nothing out here) and I'm doing quite well. As you can see from the picture, I'm married. Did you ever marry? Her name's Martha. She's a good woman and we've worked hard together for what we've got.

I expect poor old Mum is dead by now, I'm sorry she never knew how things worked out. I can imagine what she thought of me clearing off like that. I often thought of her but it was a long time before I got on my own feet and I didn't want to write her any hard luck stories after what I'd done to her.

If you didn't marry you must be on your own now so why don't you come out here and join Martha and me? I mean, you can come and have a look and if you like it, stay. Martha and me have got a bit put by and we could easily send you your ticket.

What do you say, Moses? – Martha and me would be

delighted to see you again and I'd like the chance to make things up between us.

I know it may seem silly writing to you, as far as I can remember you couldn't read when I left home, but maybe you've taught yourself by now. There wasn't much you couldn't manage if you set your mind to it. Even if you haven't I hope you'll recognise the photograph and get somebody to read it to you.

Write soon and let us know if you can come, either way we'd be pleased to hear from you.

Hoping you are keeping well,
Joe and Martha.'

I put the letter down on the table. Moses was staring into the fire. He passed his hand across his eyes, I think he'd been crying while I read the letter, I hadn't liked to look.

I glanced at the photographs. It was hard to connect the little boy with blond curls I'd seen in the sepia photographs in the family bible with the balding, jolly looking man who had his arm round an equally jolly, grey-haired lady with rosy cheeks, although I could see he was a younger version of Moses.

'I'd often wondered how he'd made out,' Moses said at last. 'Joe he signed himself, did he? Mam would have belted him for that, she always insisted on Joseph.'

'Why did you never get anyone to read you the letter?' I had decided to tackle the subject now that the letter had revealed his secret.

'You know how it is,' he shifted uncomfortably in his chair, 'none of us is very good at admitting we can't do a thing. Lots of the older people know because I was at school with them, but not the younger ones.'

'Didn't they teach you at school?'

'When I was there, they did. You must remember how short of money we were. There were all kinds of jobs going. Everything from crow scaring to stone picking. Mam needed every penny we could get after Dad died. We may have had a roof over our heads but we still had to fill our bellies.'

'Didn't they chase you when you were off school?'

'Sometimes. I remember once I was stone picking for the young Squire . . . .'

'Stone picking?'

'Yes,' Moses replied impatiently, 'picking stones out of the field so as not to harm the plough blade. Anyway, I was picking stones when Joseph ran up the lane to warn me Gaffer Roberts, our headmaster, had heard I was in the fields and was coming up to see for himself shortly. By the time he came past on his bicycle Joseph and I were over the hills and gone.'

'But your schooling suffered?'

'I wouldn't say that. Mind you, we were lucky to get free schooling, Mam had to pay a penny a week when she was a girl, and they couldn't always find it.'

'How old were you when you left?'

'Thirteen. I was glad to leave and get to work. Joseph wasn't, he'd have stayed on if he could, he was always the bright one,' he puffed reflectively at his old pipe. 'Read me the other letter, will you?'

I unfolded the second letter which was much shorter than the previous one, just a single sheet of paper with no photograph.

'Dear Moses,

I'm writing just in case my first letter went astray. I thought I could make things right between us after all these years. Even if you can't accept our offer of a visit we would like to hear how things are.

I keep reading in the papers that England's all built up these days with motorways and housing estates. They surely haven't built in our valley, have they? There I go, I still think of it as 'our' valley, even after all these years!

Martha and me often talk about you and I'd be happier in my mind if I knew that you didn't bear me a grudge because I left you in the lurch.

Hope you are well,

Joe and Martha.'

'Silly, old fool,' he said after a long pause, 'fancy him thinking I bore him a grudge after all these years. Not that I wasn't a bit bitter at first. I was the eldest and, by rights, I should have had first choice but he didn't wait to find out.'

'But, Moses, if you didn't answer these letters he must still think you *do* bear him a grudge.'

'No,' said Moses shaking his head emphatically, 'he wouldn't be so soft.'

'What else can he think? He expected you to get someone to read the letters to you and he's been waiting all this time for a reply. He didn't know you were just going to stick them in *Tom Sawyer* and forget about them.'

'I looked at the snaps. I could tell he was married. Nice looking woman, did you say her name was Martha? Mam would have liked that. I could see he was all right, so I didn't bother with the rest.'

'I could write a letter for you,' I offered eagerly.

'What?'

'You could tell me what to put, I could write it for you. Tell him everything's all right. You could even take up his offer and fly to Australia.'

'Do what? I'll do no such thing! I've never left here yet and I don't intend to go up in one of those things at my time of life.'

'You might like it,' I couldn't resist the picture of Moses eating caviar as he hurtled through the stratosphere. 'But even if you don't go, I still think you should write.'

'I wouldn't know what to say.'

'I've got some paper and a pen upstairs,' I shouted, and ran upstairs to collect it before Moses had a chance to change his mind. I drew a chair up to the table so that I got a better light from the oil-lamp and felt like one of those scribes they used to have in monasteries.

'I don't know what to put,' he protested.

'We'll do it together.'

It was gone midnight by the time a version that satisfied both of us had been hammered out. It was worse than trying to agree a statement at a summit conference. Moses sat biting his thumb for inspiration, barking out odd words and then dismissing them. I made suggestions which he scoffed at and then later accepted almost believing they were his ideas in the first place.

As I wrote the finished version out he sat on the opposite side of the table never taking his eyes off the movements of my pen urging me on like a jockey trying to get his mount past the finishing post.

'You're not changing nothing, are you?' he would ask from time to time and I had to promise I wasn't before he'd let me get on with it.

When it was finished I passed the pen across for him to sign it.

'I can't do that!' he protested.

'Well, I can't sign it for you. Come on, you hold the pen and I'll guide your hand.'

'I could put a cross, my Dad did that, my Mam told me.'

'Well, you aren't going to. Come on!'

I grabbed his hand and thrust the pen into it. He couldn't have held it more awkwardly if I'd given him a fan to hold, but eventually the spidery letters of his name were added to the bottom of the letter.

'Read it through again.'

'Dear Joseph,

You may be surprised to hear from me after all this time but circumstances have prevented me from reading your letters until now. I have got a friend staying with me at the moment and he is writing down what I want to say.

It was very kind of you to offer me the chance of a trip to Australia but I think I'm too old to take advantage of it now, much as I would like to see you again and meet your wife, Martha, who looks a very nice woman.

Mother died some years back now and I still live in the same cottage on my own.

Joseph, I don't bear you any ill will. Maybe all those years ago I might have felt differently if we'd met, but now what's done is best forgotten. I'm glad you wrote to say what you did, I appreciate that very much and I'm glad things all turned out well for you both,

Hope you are well,

Moses.'

He stretched out his hand for the letter and I thought for a moment he was going to tear it up or something but he didn't. Instead he sat studying it with the sort of reverence normally reserved for the Dead Sea Scrolls.

'What about your letter? – You said you were going to write home. They can both be posted together then.'

While he continued to gaze with wonder at his letter, including a little ill-concealed pride about his own name at the bottom, I wrote a brief note to my mother and father. It had to be brief, if it wasn't going to be a novel, so I just put, 'Dear Mum and Dad, I am quite well, don't bother to look for me any more, Peter.' Then, as an afterthought and more for Mum than Dad, I added, 'Sorry to have worried you.'

'That didn't take long,' Moses said as I sealed the envelope down.

'There wasn't much to say,' I said quietly and slipped his letter into an envelope in case he wanted to sit admiring it all night.

'I'll post those tomorrow,' he said.

Exhausted, my eyes sore from the effort of trying to see in that poor light, I followed him upstairs. No doubt Moses went to sleep to dream about his letter flying to Australia, but I lay awake reading, and rereading, Susan's letter and wishing that things could have turned out differently.

Chapter 12

'*I* POSTED them,' Moses proudly announced on his return.
'You put mine in the letter-box yourself, you didn't just hand
it across the counter?' I asked, anxious that everyone in the
district shouldn't find out where I was.

'Course I did,' Moses said scornfully, 'good job I did too, they
wanted to know all about Joseph and Australia. Costs a fortune
to send a letter there you know.'

'It would have been cheaper if we'd used an air letter. Maybe
we will next time.'

'I got a battery for the radio too.'

'I'll fix it,' I offered, suddenly remembering the wires I'd
deliberately disconnected.

'Don't worry,' he said, 'I'm more used to it than you are.'

I knew it wouldn't work but I sat patiently and watched him
fit the battery and then sit back perplexed when nothing
happened.

'Damned modern inventions!' he cursed as he poked about the
vast, dusty insides of the set with a kitchen knife.

'Modern! That set was old when I was born. They have
transistors now. Radios smaller than a match-box, the age of the
silicon chip is with us.'

'And what will that do for us?'

'One silicon chip will do the work of hundreds of men.'

'Oh, yes,' he cocked an eyebrow at me, 'and what will the men
do?'

'The Leisure Age is just around the corner.'

'I thought it had already arrived for some,' he muttered sarcastically.

'That knife's got butter on it! Come on, let me have a go.' I managed to get the set away from him so that he couldn't see what I was doing and pretended to find the loose connections. 'Ah, this is where the trouble is. Two wires have rotted through.'

'Damned thing! Just when I've bought a new battery for it too!'

'It's all right. I can fix it. Have you got any insulating tape?' I knew it was a silly question almost as soon as I asked it.

'Any what?'

'Have you got any sticking plaster then?' He found some and I bound it round the connections. 'It's a good job it's only a battery set or we'd all fry, what with you poking round in it with a buttery knife and me using sticking plaster!'

'It works best over there under the clock.'

I carried it back and switched it on. It worked like magic. Almost exactly like real magic. Disembodied sounds came wafting through the ether accompanied by a series of howls, pops and other sundry explosions.

'I suppose you realise the BBC has millions of pounds worth of highly sophisticated equipment making the sounds at their end?'

'Doesn't sound up to much to me.'

'It might work better with an aerial.'

I found a spare bit of wire and jammed it into the aerial socket with a broken bit of matchstick then hung the free end over the clock. After that it worked a little better, but not much, and always managed to receive Radio Three better than any other station. That evening after our meal we sat down and listened to an erudite talk on 'Interesting Pots from the Tang Dynasty'.

It was perhaps as well the radio was working again because we had both entered a phase of waiting. I was waiting to see if anything happened as far as Susan was concerned and Moses waited for his letter to be answered. He knew, as well as I did, that it might take ages for him to receive a reply but that didn't stop him standing by the kitchen window every morning waiting for the red post van to make its run along the main road.

From that window it looked the size of a matchbox toy but his eyes never missed it once and if it should turn up the lane towards the Baileys' he would stop whatever he was doing and rush down to the farm to see if there had been a reply. Needless to say there wasn't and so that evening he would return all gloomy and the whole process would be repeated the following day.

My letter to my parents got a much quicker reply. The first day, while Moses was out at work, I heard it mentioned on the news that they'd received the letter at home: that pleased me but the rest didn't.

'Police have renewed attempts to find Peter now that they know he hasn't left the county.'

I switched the set off and after that I made sure we missed the news broadcasts whenever Moses was around. At the same time, though, I hoped Susan had heard it because then she would know that I'd kept my promise to her. The real problem was that it meant I would have to delay my departure again.

When the argument about Susan and me had come up I had almost made my mind up to leave. I think I stayed mainly because I didn't want Susan to think Charlie was right about my character, and I wanted her to realise that I was serious about her. Now I didn't have the option. If it was on radio then it was probably on television as well and my face would be instantly recognisable again as soon as I set foot off the place. The time when I could safely leave had been moved further away again.

As we both waited impatiently for time to pass the radio became a great comfort. At home I'd been used to using the radio as a background for my other activities. I'd have it on whether I was reading a book, doing my homework or whatever, but Moses wouldn't have that when he was in the house.

'If we're going to have that thing on,' he said, 'let's listen to it.'

Consequently he wouldn't have it on during meals and when it was on we sat in total silence and listened properly. At first I found that a strain and I'd reach out for a newspaper or a book to read while the programme was on, but Moses gave me such testy looks that I soon gave that up, and eventually I grew used to his way.

As the papers arrived two days late from the farm we had to take pot luck on the programmes we heard. Moses liked classical music, but not modern, and plays, especially if they were set in a foreign country or if they were historical; but most of all he liked talks or documentaries.

'Something you can get your teeth into!' he'd exclaim, although often after we'd sat through a programme for three-quarters of an hour he promptly denounced it as rubbish as soon as it ended.

That was another curious thing. As soon as the programme ended he would get up to switch the set off, just as if the curtain had come down in a theatre. It was quite difficult to persuade him to listen to two or more consecutive programmes.

It was one night after the set had been switched off that we became aware of two mice sitting on the kitchen table watching us. Moses pulled his boot off and threw it at them. He broke three cups and a marmalade jar but missed the mice completely.

'We'll have to do something about those,' he said, and taking the storm lantern went off down the yard to return with a dozen mousetraps.

'I thought they didn't bother you?'

'I can just stand so much; when they get that cheeky it's time to do something about it.'

He cut some bits of cheese to bait the traps and then started crawling around on his hands and knees setting them up.

'Don't you think we ought to have one by the dresser? After all that's where we keep most of the food?' I suggested. 'And what about one near the end of the range?'

'Look, if you think you can do this job better than me, set some traps of your own,' he said and threw me half of the traps.

From that moment the Great Mousing Contest was born. Lacking Moses' experience I wasn't very successful at first, despite all my good ideas. It seemed they took my cheese and ended up in his traps, but after a little practice I learnt the art of setting the traps very lightly and caught more as a result. The numbers involved bothered me, though, and no matter how many we killed there still seemed to be plenty about.

'Moses,' I said one day when once again we'd come down to find almost all the traps full, 'why don't we use poison? It'd be a good deal quicker in the end.'

'What I can't do with skill, I won't do with force,' was his only reply.

The mousing contest showed how much my attitude to country living had changed during the time I had spent with Moses. When I'd first arrived I wasn't at all keen on sharing the house with mice on any terms, and I'd always insisted on taking the lantern with me to the outside lavatory even when the moon was shining. I wanted to know what kind of things I was treading on and what sort of spiders landed on my bare legs!

But now, emptying mousetraps and washing spiders out of the sink seemed the most natural thing in the world and had become part of the everyday tasks like trimming oil-lamps, winding the well, feeding pigs or even flattening tin cans and burying them in the garden.

I was even beginning to recognise some of the birds which flew past. Until Moses had pointed out the difference to me, there had only been two kinds, brown ones (all of which I called sparrows) and the rest. I still had a lot to learn though.

One night we were listening to a concert on the radio. It was Elgar's Violin Concerto and it had just reached a very quiet part near the end when suddenly Moses leapt out of his chair and went to the window. He pulled the curtains apart and then beckoned me to join him.

When my eyes got used to the light I got a glimpse of a corgi dog trotting off round the end of the building.

'Odd seeing a corgi out here,' I said.

'Corgi?' Moses laughed so much I thought his collar stud would fly out. 'That's a fox cub and unless I'm much mistaken its mother won't be far away.'

We went upstairs to look out of one of the bedroom windows

and sure enough, over by the chicken-house, we could see another figure slinking away into the darkness and by then the chickens were making enough uproar to drown the strains of Elgar.

'They're such beautiful creatures,' I said innocently, 'I can't think why anyone would want to kill them.'

'You might if you saw the damage they can do,' Moses said grimly and, almost to prove his words, a couple of nights later we heard another uproar from the hen-house. We went out to find one hen missing and six others with their heads bitten off and badly mauled. There was blood and feathers everywhere and I realised that perhaps I wasn't as used to country living as I'd thought.

Only a couple of days after that we were having breakfast and there was a sharp knock at the door. It took us both by surprise, neither of us had heard anyone cross the yard. I assumed it was the long awaited postman (it wasn't until later I remembered Susan saying he never came up to the cottage) and hid.

Through the crack of the parlour door I heard Moses open the back door and then there was conversation.

''Morning, Squire,' a man said in a high-pitched, sing-song, Black Country accent. He certainly didn't sound like a postman.

''Morning,' Moses sounded curt.

'I was just passing through . . . .'

'Where to? This road only goes up to the wood.'

'See what you mean,' the man giggled nervously and then gathered himself together. 'I meant I was passing through the village and I thought I'd call on a few selected people. I'm an antique dealer.'

'You look more like a bookie,' Moses said grimly and I had to put my hand over my mouth to stop myself laughing out loud.

'I just wondered if you'd like me to have a look round and see if you've got any nick-nacks that I could make you an offer for.'

'No, I wouldn't,' Moses' voice was firm but I could hear a note of irritation creeping into it. 'I've got nothing of value.'

'Ah, but that's the point!' the man slid into top gear of what was obviously a much used spiel. 'It takes an experienced eye to recognise these things. There's many a person I've called on who thought they'd got nothing valuable until I pointed it out to them.'

'Well, I haven't.'

'No harm in looking anyway. I can spare the time and I dare say you could use the money.'

I almost flinched at that remark. No doubt he'd found many people who were glad of a windfall but if Moses said his things were worthless then to him they were and that was the end of it.

'If you don't take your foot out of my door,' Moses said in a low threatening voice, 'I'll get my gun and make sure you do.'

'Now, there's no need to get upset,' whined the dealer.

'I'm not upset, but you soon will be.'

It was the first I'd heard that Moses had a gun and although I thought the man was bringing everything on himself I didn't want Moses getting into trouble. Anyone who didn't draw their pension might not realise there was a law that stopped people blowing other people's heads off. I decided it was time to intervene.

I threw the parlour door open in time to see Moses climbing down off a chair near the dresser, clutching an old double barrelled shot-gun, and a thin man in a bright check suit was just running out through the door. Antique dealer he might have been but he didn't seem to have an interest in old weapons. He ran across the yard, hotly pursued by Moses.

They were both out of sight when there was a loud explosion and, taking into account the age of the gun, it was a toss-up whether Moses had shot the man or the gun had blown up in his face. It was like being in a real, live Western. The difference being the bodies around here had real blood in them.

Eventually Moses returned red in the face and grinning broadly.

'You haven't shot him, have you?'

'No,' Moses shook his head, still laughing, 'but I gave him a good fright. He won't come up here again in a hurry.'

'When was that thing last fired?'

'Just before you came. I still take a few rabbits with it or a

100

pigeon or two,' he wiped it down fondly with a piece of oily rag he'd found amongst the clutter of the breakfast table. I still hadn't managed to tidy his habits up that much. 'I've had this gun years, but don't you mention it to anyone. People make a fuss about guns these days.'

'Mention it to anyone? I should think half the district heard that thing go off.'

'Only gamekeepers listen for guns and if they aren't on their land they'll take no notice.'

I only ever saw that gun once more and that was a long time off yet.

Chapter 13

When Easter came the whole valley changed. In the city I doubt if I would have noticed but out there everything was different.

Buds were appearing on the trees and hedgerows, the grass seemed a brighter green and the whole of the orchard was a white canopy of damson blossom. Even the air smelt different. Considering how sophisticated we think humans have got it's odd how something as primeval as the arrival of spring can still affect us!

We plunged our hands into the black earth, planting seeds and reaffirming our belief in the future. At school nature and the countryside had mostly seemed just poetry to me. Wordsworth's daffodils. Wordsworth never got the same kick out of his daffodils as I got out of planting peas and beans and waiting for the green shoots to appear. The rich smell of the earth warming up under the spring sun is something I shall never forget about that time.

One job I never shared with Moses was the tending of his bees. They lived in white hives right at the end of the garden and as far as I was concerned, they could stay there!

We were hard at work in the garden one day, the sun was warm on the back of my neck, when I heard footsteps coming up the path. They were too close for me to escape to the house. What I still feared most, being caught in the open, had happened at last. I straightened my back and waited, resigned and clutching at the hope that whoever it was might not recognise me.

It was Susan.

I thought I'd remembered what she looked like but as she stood there, the wind drifting strands of her corn coloured hair across her face, I realised I hadn't. She was grinning sheepishly at me but at the same time she looked very vulnerable, as if she was afraid that Moses or I would send her away. We exchanged greetings in almost a whisper but I could see that her eyes were on Moses at the moment.

'I told Dad I was coming up to see you,' she said. Her voice sounded odd but familiar.

'Thanks very much!' said Moses and thrust his spade fiercely back into the earth.

'He said it was all right as long as you were here.'

'So, I'm to be your chaperon now, am I?'

'Oh, come on, you grumpy old man. I've been coming up to see you ever since I was born. I don't see why I should stop now.'

'I don't flatter myself it's me you've come to see,' said Moses still digging.

'I'll make us some coffee. Are there any of your special ginger biscuits? They're what I really came for!'

'Get off with you!' said Moses, but I could see that she'd won him round. He'd always been proud of those biscuits which he made from a recipe of his mother's. 'They're in the airtight tin with the picture of the Queen on it.'

'I'll come and help you,' I said, quickly dusting the soil off my hands.

'Don't you two be long. I want you where I can keep an eye on you if I'm to be answerable to your father.'

Together we walked into the cool silence of the cottage. For a second we stood looking at each other, neither quite sure what the other was feeling, but when I held out my arms Susan moved easily into them and we kissed. I didn't even notice she was still wearing her glasses.

'I've missed you,' I whispered into her ear as I smelt the sleek freshness of her hair.

'Me too!'

After a moment she gently eased me away and began to make the coffee.

'We mustn't stay in here long or Moses will come glowering round,' she tipped the coffee into three large mugs. 'Did you really miss me? I nearly went crazy. At first I didn't think I'd mind *very* much, not seeing you, but it got worse and worse until I couldn't concentrate on anything.'

'I wanted to come and see you, but I didn't for your sake. I knew your Dad would make it hell for you if I did, as well as getting the police on to me.'

'I still wanted you to come, though, in a way,' she stopped what she was doing, her eyes went dreamy and her head tilted back. 'They always do in books. The hero risks everything to visit the heroine locked away in the secret tower.'

'That's all right in books,' I said ruefully, 'but even in books he gets his come-uppance.'

'But it always comes out right in the end.'

'But how far away are we from the end?'

'I bathed in the stuff that usually brings men to your window on white chargers but nothing happened,' she tried to carry on the joke.

'How far off is the end?' I repeated, I couldn't joke about it any longer. 'Light years or next week?'

'I know, love,' she said dropping the pretence. As she called me 'love' something inside me melted like butter on a hot day. She looked wistful and vulnerable again. 'Come on, let's take the coffee outside before I drown you in my tears like Alice.'

We kissed again, she collected the celebrated biscuit tin and I carried the tray out into the sunshine. I felt six foot tall, which I couldn't be even with stack heels, and just a little foolish as well.

Moses stopped work when he saw us coming and we sat on the bench to drink the coffee.

'So, what, as if I need to ask, brings you up here?' Moses looked straight at Susan.

'It's the school holidays and I felt in need of your company,' Susan grinned at him.

'Pull the other one, it's got bells on! What I meant was how did you get round your Dad?'

'You grumpy old man, you don't deserve a surprise.'

'I'll surprise you, young lady. I'll tip you over my knee and tan your hide, big as you are, if you don't watch your manners.'

Susan simply giggled back at him. She could get away with murder with him.

'Shut your eyes and hold out your hand,' she ordered. 'Go on, do as I say, or you'll never find out what I've got for you.'

Moses reluctantly did as she told him and Susan slipped an airmail envelope out of her jeans pocket and carefully placed it across his muddy hand.

He knew exactly what it was before he opened his eyes but, when he did, he didn't move he just stared at it, wide-eyed. I thought for a moment he was going to cry but he didn't. Instead he turned the envelope over and over. By the time he'd finished he'd examined the writing on the front and the back, as well as the stamp, a hundred times.

'Don't you think you'd better open it?' I asked impatiently. 'You've waited long enough for it, for heaven's sake let's find out what it says!'

He quietly handed the envelope to Susan. 'You do it, my hands are shaking too much.'

Carefully she slit the envelope and pulled out a single sheet of paper, as she did a dog barked on the far side of the valley and a single black crow flapped lazily across the blue skies above us.

'Go on, Susan,' I urged, 'read it out.'

'Dear Moses,' she began, 'Thank you for your letter. I understand about the delay, but I'm sorry to have to tell you that your letter arrived too late. Joseph died two years ago. He'd had a bit of trouble for a while but then he suffered a heart attack from which he never recovered.

He'd always worried about what you thought of him. It had preyed on his mind for years, but he was determined not to write until he'd got himself set up. That was his way. He really wanted to be able to offer you the chance to visit us. I'm sure that he would have been very relieved to hear that you bore no ill will towards him.

I'm sorry that we shan't ever meet, Joe told me so much about you and the valley, but I'm glad to hear that you are well. I'm only sorry that I have to send you bad news in return.' Susan slowly folded the letter and put it back in its envelope. 'It's signed "Martha".'

None of us said another word for some time. The eager smile of anticipation had drained from Moses' face after the third line and now he sat, staring at the mud of the garden as it dried on his boots in the heat from the sun. I couldn't think of anything to say which would comfort him. I knew that he'd waited so anxiously for this letter, overjoyed at the idea of straightening everything out with his brother, now all that was ended.

At last he took the letter from Susan's outstretched hand. Without a word he thrust it into the bib pocket of his overalls and went back to digging the garden.

Susan and I watched him from the corners of our eyes.

'Poor old Moses,' she said.

'He'd waited for so long,' I nodded, 'maybe I shouldn't have interfered. I should have realised all those years had passed. I just didn't think anything as drastic as that would have happened. I only wanted to do something for him after all he's done for me.'

'You weren't to know,' she rested her cool hand on mine, the skin was already browning from the sun and I noticed the fine, short, delicate hairs had bleached white around her wrist. 'Don't blame yourself, Peter.'

During the Easter holiday Susan found several good excuses to get up to the cottage but only when she knew Moses was there so that we couldn't be accused of doing anything wrong.

It was a long time before Moses mentioned the letter from his brother's wife and even then he didn't do it directly. We were standing in the orchard and Moses was trying to decide if he could smell frost or not.

'We get a decent crop of damsons one year in eight,' he mumbled to himself. 'The rest of the years the frost takes the blossom.'

106

'Not much you can do about it then.'

'The Old Vicar used to light little bonfires under the trees to keep the frost from settling. Don't know myself though,' he slapped the gnarled trunk of one of the trees and then turned to give me a thoughtful look. 'Have you decided what you're going to do yet?'

'Not really. The letter home stirred things up a bit, I'll have to wait for that to quieten down first.'

'Don't leave it too late,' he said quietly. I could tell that he still had Joseph on his mind. 'Some things ought to be made up. An open wound only festers. It's none of my business what went on at your house but I remember Joseph going and I know how your Mum must feel.'

We walked silently back to the house through the gathering gloom. The light from the lamp spilled out into the yard and the cottage looked warm and inviting. Above us the moon hung, wreathed in silver mist.

'Just don't leave things too long, that's all lad.'

'Do you think there is going to be a frost then?'

'Like most things, we'll know for sure by morning.'

When Susan came up to the house she would often sit on the bench in the sun and watch us work in the garden. Sometimes she would bring a book she was studying for her exam and it gave me a curious feeling of nostalgia.

'I just accepted books at school,' I told her, 'but not having studied now for months in a way I miss them. The only reading I do now is for pleasure, old books of Moses'.'

'Do you think you could go back to studying again? Pick up where you left off?'

'I don't know,' I sighed. 'I tell myself that it would be dead easy, but really I'm not so sure. I still think sometimes that I just ought to go back home and make the best of things but I can't quite make myself do it.'

'Your Mum would be pleased, even if your Dad wouldn't. I'll never forget seeing your Mum on television the night your note arrived, she looked that excited.'

'That was your doing,' I reminded her and gave her arm a squeeze. 'I never would have written that but for you, not after all that time.'

'You can still go back, Peter. It isn't too late.'

I bit my bottom lip and I could feel my face creased in a frown. 'I just want to make something of myself. I just want to try.'

Chapter 14

*T*HE frost didn't take the damson blossom and as spring ambled into summer we found the small, hard, green fruit lurking under the leaves. Tractors droned round the fields like flies round jam as they cut the lush, deep, green grass for silage. The banks of the track to the wood were edged with white umbrellas of cow parsley and under the trees, on the edge of the wood, lay misty beds of bluebells who's scent hung heavy on the evening air.

When I walked that track I walked it alone. Susan was back at school and visits, even on the pretext of seeing Moses, were utterly banned. The evenings were long now, it often stayed light until gone ten, I could never remember it doing that when I lived in the city but perhaps the street lights accounted for my not noticing.

After our evening meal, instead of sitting in front of the fire with the radio, we went out and worked in the garden. Picking, planting and hoeing until owls swooped down from the wood and it was too dark for us to see.

Although Moses was busy helping Charlie Bailey he never missed the weekly bus that went into the nearby market town.

'We haven't picked enough peas!' he shouted as he stuffed the produce into two huge wicker baskets. 'And did you remember to get the parsley?'

'It's on the draining board,' I said wearily. We'd been up since five that morning so that everything would be fresh for the shops.

At half past eight on the dot Moses would set out, staggering under the weight of the baskets, to trudge down the lane to the main road for the bus. At half past four I would see him coming back up the lane and always made sure the kettle was boiling.

'Robbers!' he'd snarl as he collapsed, red faced, into his chair. When he'd recovered his breath he'd continue his attack on the local traders. 'Want all the money for themselves. I grow the stuff but they make more than I do. Money for old rope!'

'Why do it then?'

'Got to make a bit somehow; I can't make enough going round the houses.'

That was what he did most evenings for the rest of the week. Anything he couldn't take to market he sold at the cottages and new brick bungalows dotted around the valley.

'Too lazy to grow it themselves and want me to do all the work,' he grumbled one night when he came back with a huge order for peas from one of the new houses. 'Want peas for their freezer, or something.'

'That's good, isn't it?'

'They want them shelled!'

The next night we sat down and shelled a mountain of peas but he came back grinning from ear to ear when he'd delivered them. 'I made them pay,' was all he said but I could tell that they'd regret their laziness.

Not knowing much about food, except the sort of thing you buy in tins, boxes or bags at the supermarket, I had no idea what was in store for me. As the season wore on there was more and more work to do. Lettuce to trim, radishes to wash and bunch, and then, if that wasn't enough, Moses started to make jam of everything he could lay his hands on.

Instead of struggling back from market days with empty baskets they would now be piled with bags of sugar. How he made it up the hill sometimes I just don't know.

Night after night he would stand at the range stirring the contents of a huge brass jam kettle with a wooden spoon, and the next day the house would be alive with bees and wasps who had come scavenging for the pickings.

110

'It's all laziness,' he muttered like an old wizard gleefully mixing up a spell in his cauldron. 'Laziness' was his word throughout the summer! 'They could make any of this stuff themselves, but the young ones don't bother! It would break my mother's heart to see what they let go to waste these days.'

'Why go to the trouble of making the jam for them then?'

'Because,' he said, giving me a huge, knowing wink, 'I get twice as much for the jam as I would for the fruit!'

Sometimes I left him bottling the latest concoction and went out into the warm evening air of the yard. The sweet, dark smell of new mown hay drifted up from the farm below and enveloped me like a freshly opened packet of tobacco. Although it was dark I could still hear the steady drone of tractors working in the fields, using their headlights to take advantage of the last hours of the day. It seemed as if the whole valley were taking part in some vast, urgent race and yet I seemed to remain detached from it all. Although I helped Moses in every way I could I was still a bystander and even, on occasions, felt a little in the way.

Somewhere in the wood, behind me, an owl screeched. Another answered. Then a fox barked but there was no answer to that cry. By now I recognised these things readily but it still didn't make me part of the life out there and I longed for someone of my own age to talk to, especially Susan.

The harvest season began to take its toll on Moses. Working hard in the fields all day and then tramping round the village with his baskets each evening left him looking drained under his mahogany coloured skin.

'It's the pull up the hill that does it,' he said as he flopped down in the chair, breathless and exhausted.

'It's too much for you at your age,' I protested.

'Nonsense!' he said angrily, but I could see he was too out of breath to continue.

'I wish I could go for you, but I daren't be seen round here. Somebody would be certain to recognise me. Susan could though,' I suggested. My suggestion wasn't exactly unselfish!

'I wouldn't hear of it. Nor would Charlie.'

111

I let the matter drop but it worried me to see Moses getting worse as the week wore on and I was relieved when he came back and told me that he had spoken to Charlie at last.

'What did he say?' I asked eagerly.

'He said she could . . . .'

'Great!'

'. . . as long as it doesn't interfere with her homework. He said he doesn't want a drop-out in his family!'

'Still getting at me, well I don't care.'

'She'll only be coming up two or three evenings at the most and remember, she's coming for my benefit not yours!' he said firmly, but I could see a twinkle in his eye.

'How's self-sufficiency suiting you now, then?' she said when she came to collect the baskets.

'Sometimes I think if I see another lettuce, cucumber, or pot of jam, I'll slit my throat,' I grinned. She looked great. 'But I think I'll survive, if Moses does.'

'Dad says he'll kill himself if he isn't careful. That's the only reason he's letting me do this. Greatly against his better judgement, so he says.'

She swung off down the path and I was left, longing to go with her, counting the time as I waited for her return with the money and the empty baskets.

'You don't have to come up with them at this time,' Moses said the first night she returned. 'It'd do when you next come.'

'It's no trouble,' she laughed at him.

'Don't you two get me in trouble with Charlie!'

'We won't, don't worry,' she said quietly. Those few stolen moments in the warm summer evening air were the best part of the day.

It wasn't long before the fields in the valley were turning gold with crops of wheat and barley which swished under the slightest breath of wind, like a golden tide being washed on to a sea-shore. Susan was on holiday now but any hope that I would see more of her was firmly dashed.

'No, Peter. He says I can come up a couple of evenings to deliver Moses' stuff to the village, but that's it.'

112

'Nice to be liked.'

'You can't blame him,' she said softly, snuggling into my arms, 'he doesn't know you as well as I do. But then, if he did, he probably wouldn't let me come at all!'

Suddenly she slid away from me and stood leaning on the yard wall looking out over the quiet valley. Smoke was drifting in straight lines from the chimneys of the houses and the evening air felt cool after the heat of the day.

'Sometimes I wish you'd never come here,' she said gently.

'Thanks!'

'It's just that nothing will ever be the same again. I've been coming up here for years to see Moses. When you're gone and I come I shall always think of you being here. I shan't be able to stay away because I'd miss seeing Moses, and yet at the same time I won't want to come because of the memories.'

'I haven't said I'm going yet.'

'No, but you will, one day.'

'I like it round here. Maybe I should stay and become part of it.'

'No,' she shook her head. 'You never could. To you this is just a game of let's pretend. You couldn't live like Moses for the rest of your life.'

'Lots of people do. Communes, things like that. The Alternative Society.'

'Or, as my Dad says, drop-outs! No, Peter, this isn't you. You make a good show of it and you've worked hard, but somewhere there's something waiting for you to do.'

'I just wish *I* knew what it was.'

'You will, one day.'

'Are you two going to be out there all night?' Moses shouted through the open door.

I watched her until she went out of sight around the bend in the path and then went back in to join Moses. Maybe she was right, but just at the moment I was satisfied with what I'd got.

'I can see why you want to work in the city, but you wouldn't want to go and live in one, would you?' I asked her the next evening. There was less stuff coming out of the garden now and

113

nothing for her to take to the village. We were stretched out lazily on the bench while poor old Moses pounded up and down the garden encouraging things to grow more quickly.

'I think I would, for a while anyway. The country's all right but you haven't lived here all your life. All the things you take for granted, cinemas, discos, shops even, they're all ten miles from here. You just used to walk down the street, I'll bet. If I want to go I have to get Mum or Dad to drive me. Usually in the summer they're too busy. Look at it now, harvest on, no chance! The country's all right as long as you've got the means of getting out. Kids haven't.'

'Haven't you got a bike?'

'You can't cycle ten miles back from the cinema at half-past ten at night, you clown.'

'I don't much miss cinemas and discos. I did at first but I don't now.'

'That's probably because you've lived with them on your doorstep for most of your life. The novelty would wear off if you *had* to stay here.'

'I might yet,' I tried to reassure her. This topic came up in every conversation now. Sometimes, like now, it was jokey but underneath it was serious and I tried like mad to convince us both.

'There's nothing to keep you.'

'There's you.'

'You'll soon forget me,' although her lips smiled as she spoke her eyes were clouded with that vulnerable uncertainty that I remembered from our first meetings.

'No, I won't.'

'Kiss me, then,' she said and I did.

A sudden shout from the garden made us leap apart. At first we thought Moses was angry that we had the gall to kiss in front of him but when we looked round there was no sign of him. Eventually there was another call. A wordless, pleading sound this time which seemed to come from the tall rows of runner beans.

We found him lying full length on the earth beneath the

114

spade-shaped leaves of the beans; the bright orangey red flowers seemed to mock him as he lay helpless, his watery eyes pleading with us. The scuff marks by the toes of his boots and the mud on his elbows suggested that he had been trying to drag himself towards the house.

'If we each put an arm under his we should be able to carry him back to the house,' I said. Even upright his legs didn't seem to function.

When we had got him onto the couch he looked a deathly white and, despite the warmth of the evening, he was shivering.

'What he needs is a doctor!' I said firmly. Moses opened his eyes and moaned at us in protest. The fear showed clearly in the eyes although his protest lacked it's usual vigour.

'Peter, I'll light a fire and make him a drink. You go and get Mum, she'll know what's best.'

I sped down the lane towards the farm. In the distance I could hear a tractor and as I got to the farmyard Charlie was just turning in with a cart piled high with straw. He took one look at my winded condition and leapt off the machine without bothering to switch it off.

'What's up?' he shouted, only just resisting the temptation to grab hold of me by my jersey. 'If there's anything wrong with Susan I'll . . . .'

'No, Susan sent me to get Mrs Bailey. It's Moses, he fell over and couldn't get up. I think he's very ill.'

'Go to the house and get Madge,' he shouted to me and he went back to the tractor and began to uncouple the cart.

Mrs Bailey, a small, bird-like woman in complete contrast to Mr Bailey, darted out of the house as soon as I knocked and it was only moments before we were all three lurching up the track on the tractor leaving the cartload of straw stranded like a whale in the lane.

After Mrs Bailey had gone into the house to look at Moses, Mr Bailey, Susan and myself stood uncomfortably together in the yard. All our thoughts were on Moses, but we were uneasily aware of being together. We all stared down the garden to avoid having to look at each other and Susan stood furthest away.

'Moses said you'd helped him a lot in the garden,' Charlie said, breaking the awkward silence with a subject that should be a safe one.

'I did my best,' I was trying hard not to sound tense. 'He had to show me what to do.'

'Yes,' he gave me a disparaging glance, 'I suppose he'd have to.'

'Dad!' Susan pleaded quietly.

'You've kept things neat up here, I'll say that for you.'

'Do you think Moses will see a doctor this time?' I asked. Talking about Moses was far safer than talking about me.

'I doubt it. He reckons they'll take one look at him and bung him in a home. It was the same when he had that do just after you came. I've warned him many a time, but he won't listen. You can't make him see a doctor if he doesn't want to.'

'He should at least have a check-up,' I was torn between my concern for Moses and my fear of strangers who might recognise me coming on to the place.

'You try telling him that! I've told him often enough that with their help he could live another twenty years but his answer's always the same one. "I'll go when my time comes, but I'd rather go from here!" Then he goes and frightens us like this, obstinate old devil!'

The silence of affection that the three of us felt in our different ways for Moses was broken as Mrs Bailey came out to join us in the yard.

'How is he, Madge?'

'He's all right now, I think. He's asleep anyway. I don't think he ought to be moved upstairs. Not tonight anyway.'

'What's the matter with him, Mum?'

'I think he's had a slight stroke.'

'I was so scared. He couldn't walk and he looked so helpless. I've never seen anyone like that before.'

'Well, I think the use is coming back into his legs,' she said, putting an arm round Susan's shoulder to comfort her. 'We'll have to see how he is tomorrow.'

'Did you mention the doctor to him?'

'No, Charlie, I didn't. I didn't want him having another stroke. But if he's no better tomorrow we'll get the doctor to look at him whether Moses wants him or not. Will you be able to look after him tonight, Peter?'

'What do I have to do?'

'There isn't much you can do. I left him on the couch. Just keep an eye on him and keep him warm. You don't mind being alone with him? – I could stay if you'd like me to.' I shook my head. 'I think he'll be all right, he just needs rest.'

There was no affectionate good-night with Susan that night but as they all three turned to leave Susan turned back and gave me a slow wink that carried more than humour in it and I felt better.

For a while I stood in the yard listening to the decreasing throb of the tractor as it made its way back to the farm. At last it stopped and the night was quiet except for a single dog barking somewhere down in the valley. I turned and went into the silent kitchen.

Moses was asleep on the couch. A little of the colour had come back into his cheeks. I put another log on the fire. The flames licked it, it spat a shower of sparks, and Moses stirred for a moment in his sleep.

I collected a blanket from upstairs and threw it over myself as I settled into the armchair. Asleep his face was softer but the skin was like tissue paper and often during that night I thought about the possibility of his dying. In a way it made me think even more about my own life, and about time. Being young, life seemed very long but Moses knew, better than anyone, that life is measured and shouldn't be wasted.

Throughout the night I only dozed but when the birds began to welcome the sunrise, seeing that Moses was still sleeping peacefully, I blew out the lamp and fell into a deep, uneasy sleep myself.

Chapter 15

'It's almost like being married.' Almost a week had passed, Susan was finishing the washing up and I'd just brought in some logs I'd chopped for the fire.

Moses had recovered enough to move back to his own room but Mrs Bailey was very unhappy, while I still had so much work to do outside, about leaving him alone. Greatly against Charlie's wishes his wife had insisted that Susan came up each day to look after Moses and the house while I worked outside in the garden. Charlie Bailey had only eventually agreed to this arrangement when Mrs Bailey had threatened to come up herself if he wouldn't let Susan go. Knowing his wife's help was essential to him in the thick of the harvest he'd given in.

'I suppose we could get married,' I suggested. She looked very domesticated, an apron over her jeans and hair flopping across her eyes as she dried the dishes.

'Thanks! Don't force yourself! There's plenty who'd jump at the chance,' she tossed her head back in mock offence.

'Fine prospect I'd be,' unable to sustain the joke for long, reality always hit me. 'No home, no job, no hope!'

'You've just got to sort yourself out. You can do things if you want to,' Susan nodded her head at me to emphasize her point. No matter how many times I dropped into this mood she was always willing to take me seriously and not just brush me aside with some silly remark. 'Look at the garden out there. You'd never done anything like that before but it's a credit to you. Even Dad said that.'

118

'Moses showed me how to do it all.'

'Yes. But that's the whole point. He showed you and you learnt.'

'What do you think then,' I said brightening up, 'I ought to be a market-gardener?'

'Don't talk wet!' she said and threw the dishcloth at me.

I picked it up and went as if to rub it in her face but instead I slipped my arms round her, gave her a big bear hug, followed by a long kiss.

'Peter, stop it.' The kiss had ended and she was pulling away from me.

'What?'

'You know,' she said hooking her thumbs under her hair and running her hands down it in a characteristic gesture of uncertainty.

'No, I don't.'

'We're getting too fond of each other.'

'How can we do that?'

'One thing will just lead to another and before we know where we are . . . .' her voice trailed off for a moment, then she added, 'I'm only human, you know.'

'Only just.'

'You'd make a joke at your own funeral. The only thing you take seriously is yourself. You know very well what I mean. Up here alone all day, we're both getting ideas and it simply isn't right.'

'Why not? – We're both grown-up, we know what we're doing.'

'We're grown-up? I'm having arguments with Dad about what I'm going to do with the rest of my life when I leave school and you've opted out. None of that strikes me as particularly grown-up.'

'Things will work out,' I smiled. It was part of our relationship that as soon as one of us was depressed it was the other one's job to cheer them up.

'Don't bank on it. Things have a habit of *not* working out unless you do something to help them.'

'So, what have you decided to do?'

'Make darned certain that I at least get all the subjects I need for the course *I* want to do.'

'What about the subjects for the farming college?'

'I'll get those too.'

'Then your Dad will make you go to Agricultural College and you'll end up married to a farmer.'

'Not if I can help it. This is my life and I've decided I'm going to win that battle or bust in the attempt. I've seen what's happened to you and I'm determined not to let it happen to me.'

'Thanks.'

'You know what I mean. *I've* been hoping that if I ignored it long enough the issue would just go away. I know now it won't and I'll just have to face up to it.'

'Good for you,' I admired her courage even if I was jealous of her smugness. 'I've made a decision too.'

'Oh, what are you going to do?'

'Kiss you.'

'No, you are not. I'm going to take a cup of tea up to Moses. He must be dry as a bone.' And she did, though not quite straight away.

As I threw the midday corn to the chickens and collected the eggs from the straw-lined nestboxes, I thought over what Susan had said about us getting too fond of each other. I knew that really she was right, I was having difficulty controlling my emotions. Now that I was actually in the situation everything seemed very far removed from the dirty jokes I'd heard exchanged at school. The silly competitions when boys took girls to the cinema and compared notes the following day to see who'd got the furthest didn't seem to have anything to do with our relationship. Of course I found Susan very attractive, I didn't even notice her goggles these days, but I enjoyed her company and conversation too.

As I carried the eggs back to the house I realised that if I had left in the spring this problem wouldn't have come up. I'd have remembered Susan as somebody nice and kind who I enjoyed kissing. Now there was an ache inside me, a yearning whenever

120

we were apart and a restless feeling of dissatisfaction whenever we were together.

I transferred the eggs from my bowl into the dresser. Susan came back downstairs, the cup of tea was untouched.

'He's sleeping. I'll leave him for a bit and go up later.'

'Susan, do your Mum and Dad row all the time?'

'Only if Dad lays down the law, which isn't often. Then Mum nods at him without actually saying whether she agrees or not. Usually she does what she thinks best in the end. Nine times out of ten everything ends happily. They've had worse rows over you than they've ever had over anything else.'

'Oh?' I couldn't help sounding a little pleased. 'Why?'

'Because Mum tends to think I ought to be left alone to work things out for myself.'

'You mean she likes me?'

'I wouldn't go quite that far,' she smiled. 'She just thinks that if I want to get mixed up with you that's my business, and she's always stood up for me when Dad shouts the odds about you.'

'Really?' I couldn't quite picture that funny little bird-like creature standing up to Charlie in full flood! 'I suppose my Mum's the same. She solves her problems by keeping out of Dad's way as much as she can.'

'Were they always like that?'

'As long as I can remember.'

'Then why did they get married?'

'Why does anyone? I don't suppose she knew he was work-shy then. Maybe he wasn't, perhaps something happened to change him into what he is now.'

'Why do you think they stay together, then? They obviously, from what you say, don't love each other.'

'Perhaps they do. I remember once when Dad was ill, a real one this time, not one of his joke illnesses, Mum looked after him night and day until she wore herself out.'

'She must feel something for him then.'

'Perhaps, but it doesn't seem enough does it? All marriages can't be like that. The trouble is it's the only marriage I've lived close to and it's difficult to understand how other people live.'

121

'Look at the time!' Susan leapt up and poured another cup of tea for Moses. 'I'd better get upstairs and see how he is, then I must get home, Mum and Dad are going out tonight and I'm farm-sitting.'

'Perhaps I could sneak down and spend the evening with you. I might have my wicked way with you!'

'Terrific! Leave Moses up here on his own and probably be discovered in the height of your passion by Dad! That could really make you the most popular man in the world.' She pulled a face at me and ran off up the stairs.

A few days later Susan and I were both watching Moses blow breadcrumbs and spill tea all over the bed.

'I'm getting up tomorrow,' he announced. Susan and I both looked at each other in dismay. Whilst being thrown together produced its strain, as soon as Moses was back on his feet Charlie would probably insist on her visits ending.

'You should wait until you're properly better,' I said perhaps too hastily.

'I am. Anyway, there's things to do.'

'Nothing I can't handle.'

'The bees.'

'You win! The bees I can't handle.'

'Well, you'll have to help.'

'Moses, I'd do anything for you, anything, that is, except go near the bees.'

'I never thought I'd see a grown lad frightened of a few insects.'

'I'm not exactly frightened,' I could see Susan laughing at me out of the corner of my eye. 'They give me the creeps anyway.' Susan was laughing openly at me squirming. 'You help Moses, Susan, why don't you?'

'Oh, no,' she threw up her hands, 'not me! I'm a coward about bees, but at least I admit it.'

'Well,' said Moses, looking forlorn, 'I can't manage them on my own after all this business.'

Reluctantly, I eventually agreed and four days later, looking like urban spacemen with veils over our faces, we set off.

'The main thing is to convince yourself that you aren't frightened,' he recommended as we trudged up the orchard. I tried to increase the distance between us but he kept waiting for me.

'What happens if I don't succeed in persuading the bees I'm not frightened?'

'You'll sweat, they'll smell it and it'll upset them.'

If I look back over my relatively short life, the few hours I spent in that orchard with Moses and his bees, which relentlessly buzzed me like kamikaze pilots, seems to be longer than the rest of my life. From the moment he lifted out a frame, covered in scurrying insects wearing football jerseys on the wrong end, until he put the last roof back on the last hive, seemed like waiting for eternity. Why bee-keepers wear flimsy veils I'll never know! If ever I have anything more to do with bees, and it won't be voluntarily I can assure you, I shall be wearing full diving equipment and a glass windowed helmet.

For the next three days and nights we were under siege. Inside the cottage Moses was cranking what looked like a washing machine designed by a mad man which sent honey spurting out of the combs, while outside every bee and wasp in the district was doing its best to find a way in. No windows or doors could be left open. Even the smallest crack had been blocked with rag or paper but still they made it and I was left charging round the room swatting with a newspaper like a demented tennis player!

The first clear amber liquid that poured from the machine Moses smeared on to chunks of freshly buttered new bread and it tasted like food fit for the Gods. By the end of three days, when the whole house reeked of the stuff and everything we touched was sticky with it, I wouldn't have cared if I'd never seen honey ever again. It seemed as if the smell had permeated to the very core of me and that it would never again leave my nostrils or my hair.

At last, when it was all over we surveyed the pyramid of gold jars in the parlour.

'I'm glad that's over,' said Moses. 'There'll be a chap coming up for those in a few days. I'll get Charlie to ring from the farm.'

'Have I got to see him, Moses?' I asked. I still worried about being recognised.

'No, they'll say when they're coming and Susan can let him in.'

'That's all right then,' I tried to conceal my pleasure at the thought of seeing Susan again. Just as we'd feared, now that Moses was back on his feet, she was banned from coming up to the cottage. 'Just a minute, why won't you be here?'

'Because I'm going back to work.'

'You can't.'

'I can, everything's done up here now, apart from a few runner beans to salt down for the winter and the damsons to pick.'

'But you've been ill, very ill.'

'I can't help that, I've me job to do.'

'Charlie will send you straight home, if he's got any sense.'

'Then I'd go and work for somebody else.'

Nothing I could say made any difference. In a couple of days Moses had gone back to work and Susan and I were waiting for the man to arrive to collect the honey.

A small blue pick-up truck heaved its way up to the cottage just after midday. It was only the second vehicle I'd ever seen use that track.

I was skulking out of sight down the garden while Susan showed the man where to go.

'And how is the old gentleman?' I heard him ask.

'Oh, he's fine.'

'You'd be his daughter I suppose?'

'No, just a friend,' Susan sounded as if she might burst into giggles any minute. Anybody less like his daughter was hard to imagine, especially as she'd dressed up specially.

'I haven't seen you for so long,' she said when I whistled at her arrival, 'I wanted to look nice for you.'

She was wearing a hip-hugging pair of trousers in a light tweedy material and a blue shirt that brought out the colour of her eyes.

'You certainly succeeded,' I gasped with admiration.

124

The man put the last box into the pick-up and slammed the tailboard up.

'I'll just settle up with you then,' he said and I heard him counting to himself as he riffled through a wad of notes. 'There we are then. Thank Mr Beech for me, sorry not to have seen him, but I'll see him next year, all being well. Terrah!'

I heard the slam of the door, the engine start and soon he was off down the hill. Susan came down the path toward me. Her hip swayed out as she slightly lost her balance, the wind caught up her hair and spread it out in a fan. My stomach lurched slightly, as it often did now at the sight of her.

'You don't like bees do you?'

'No,' I said, 'and I'm glad to see the back of that honey.'

'Perhaps you ought to get to like bees.'

'Why?'

She held up a wad of notes, it wasn't very thick, but they were ten pound notes. 'How much do you think there is here?'

'I haven't a clue.'

'Four hundred pounds almost.'

'Crikey!'

'Couldn't you like bees now? – Not even a little bit?'

'Not even for four hundred pounds.'

The rest of the afternoon I didn't do any gardening and Susan didn't do any housework. Instead we spent most of the time on the couch. In the past we'd made sort of rules about where we could touch each other. In the past that had worked out, but this time, perhaps because we hadn't seen each other for a while, it didn't.

'Peter, don't,' she moaned, 'suppose Moses comes back?'

'He won't be back for ages yet.'

'He might, Peter, you don't know.'

'Come up to my room then,' I whispered.

'No, Peter, please!'

A while later we were lying back on my make-shift mattress. My arm was beneath her naked waist. We were both looking through the window at the clouds gathering in the gloom outside. In one of the apple trees a thrush was singing his repetitive song. I turned to find Susan had tears trickling down her cheeks.

'What's up love?' I ran my hand through her hair which fell back over her smooth shoulders. 'You're not sorry are you?'

'No, I'm happy. That's why I'm crying. I'm just so glad it was you, Peter,' she said quietly and kissed me on the cheek.

I went down first to make some tea and for some reason the money caught my eye. It was still lying on the kitchen table where Susan had left it.

'What are you looking at?' she said standing on the last step of the staircase.

'All that money. Four hundred pounds. We could run away together and get married with that.'

'You couldn't,' her voice barely sounded across the room.

'No,' I said, shaking my head slowly. 'I couldn't. I'd like to run away with you and to marry you, but I couldn't take that money. So, maybe I'm not like my Dad after all.'

It was going dark when we heard Moses coming up the path. We kissed briefly and Susan slipped out before he got to the yard gate.

'You're out late,' he said as he passed me in the yard.

'Just wanted a breath of air,' I said.

'Don't catch your death,' he laughed as he went into the kitchen and closed the door.

I leant on the gate and listened. I could hear Susan's footsteps growing fainter. There was a brief moment when I could no longer hear her and then one of the dogs at the farm started to bark a greeting.

Another dog further down the valley checked in and two others passed on the message until I could hear no more replies. The whole valley, or at least its dogs, knew my Susan was safely back home and it seemed to issue a contented sigh and then relapse into easy stillness.

Chapter 16

'HAVE you seen much of Susan lately?' I asked the question with difficulty, perched on a ladder and stretching out to pick two particularly luscious damsons which always seemed to grow in the most inaccessible places.

'Not for a while,' Moses said from the foot of the ladder.

Even though she had gone back to school after the holidays she had usually found time to steal away and we would walk in the woods or just sit behind a hedge and look out across the valley. I'd been frightened at first that the change in our relationship might spoil things, but it had only made our feelings for each other deeper. Our need to be together was more urgent and yet for the last week I hadn't seen her.

'That's the last tree,' Moses heaved almost as big a sigh as I did. We'd been picking all day.

I helped him carry the ladder back. Our feet scuffled the fallen gold leaves that lay beneath the trees. It smelt almost the same as a spring evening, clear and bright; but the musty smell of autumn swam up from the dead leaves as our boots crushed them.

'You get supper,' Moses said, 'I'll make a start on the damsons.'

After the honey I thought the marathons were over but I soon realised I was wrong. The buckets of dark fruit were slowly converted into jam, wine and pickles. Row upon row waited on every available shelf and window sill. I expected Susan to be

127

called back into service but nothing happened.

'Isn't Susan coming up to take these to the village?' I asked one night when I could bear it no longer.

'I mentioned it to Charlie and he said she'd said she was coming up,' Moses replied but two days later there was still no sign of her.

I knew the time the school bus dropped her at the end of the lane and the next day I set out in good time to meet her. I didn't want to bump into Charlie Bailey, as far as he knew we hadn't met since Moses had recovered, so I set out across the fields on a route I'd mapped out from the kitchen window.

Even so, I was early and I squatted down with my back against a gate-post to wait wondering what it was that had kept her away for so long. At last I heard footsteps coming up the track and cautiously looked through the hedge to make sure I wasn't going to leap out and surprise a total stranger. It was Susan. Dressed in school clothes and carrying a pile of books she *looked* almost like a stranger. I had never seen her dressed this way and, with her hair pulled back into a band at the back of her head, she looked much younger.

'Hello, Susan,' I whispered as she drew level with my gate. She was startled but without saying anything she checked that nobody was watching her before she shinned over the gate and dropped on to the grass beside me.

'Where've you been? Why haven't you been up to the cottage?'

'I've had a lot of homework. Catching up after the holidays,' she plucked at a button on her raincoat as she spoke.

'Moses wants you to take the damson stuff to the village.'

'I know.'

'He said you were coming but you didn't turn up.'

'I couldn't.'

'Why not?' I couldn't get through to her at all. It was like talking to a complete stranger.

'Oh, Peter, I wanted to come, but Mum made me promise not to or she said she'd tell Dad.' She had barely got the words out before she started to cry. It was a silent, painful crying that

128

pressed the tears through her closed eyes. I hugged her quiet and she pushed up her glasses to push away the tears with half clenched hands.

'Tell me, what is it?'

'My period's late.'

'That happens, doesn't it?'

'Not to me it doesn't. I usually get very heavy ones, so Mum notices. She asked me a week ago and I tried to put her off, but she'd already guessed. She said I wasn't to see you again or she'd tell Dad.' She shrugged. 'It looks as if he's going to have to be told anyway.'

'So, we'll have to get married,' I said, trying to keep my voice quiet but firm. Even as I spoke I knew it wasn't really that simple.

'With no money, nowhere to live, me still at school and you without a job?' Susan had had longer to think about it and was crystallizing vague thoughts that flew round my head. 'What sort of marriage would that be?'

'We love each other, we could work it out.'

'We do now, but would it survive all that and a baby as well? I'm not seventeen yet, Peter.'

'I want to look after you, make things work.'

'We've got to be sensible. You're under age, so am I. We'd need their permission to get married. My father wouldn't give his consent and you can't exactly ask yours.'

'We could run away.'

'What from Peter? – Ourselves?'

'I thought you loved me, Susan.'

'I *do*, Peter,' she almost shouted. 'And that's why, if never before, we've got to be sensible, though heaven knows it's the last thing I want to be, because when I am I get so frightened.'

The last words died away in another burst of sobbing. This time nothing I could say or do comforted her. My arms round her, her head on my chest we sat on the grass, me wishing that I could undo my mistakes, my stupidity, my selfishness.

'What's going on here?'

The voice of Charlie Bailey, who had come up the lane, split through our thoughts. Susan leapt to her feet and rubbed her eyes on her sleeve.

'Nothing, Dad.'

'You,' he said, pointing at Susan, 'get up that lane, home. I'll talk to you later.'

'It's nothing, Dad. Peter's not to blame.'

'I said no good would come of mixing with the likes of him,' he glared angrily at me as he grabbed me by the shirt and lifted a fist as big as a ham. 'If you've harmed Susan I'll not be responsible for what I'll do to you.'

'Dad, no, please!'

'If you won't go, I'll take you my girl.'

His hands dropped from me and he pushed Susan, who was half walking half running, at arms length ahead of him. I was left standing in the entrance to the field, helpless and useless. I didn't want to leave Susan to face the rows and accusations alone, and yet at the same time I knew it would have made things worse if I'd gone with them. Even supposing Charlie would let me, which seemed unlikely.

When Moses came home from work it was clear from the expression on his face that he'd heard the gist of the argument before he'd left the farm.

'You've done it now, lad!' was all he said, but it carried a wealth of meaning.

'I know.'

'So, what's your next move? If you're thinking of making a run for it, you'd best get going. Charlie was hollering blue murder when I left.'

'He threatened me already.'

'The police is the best you can expect. What are you going to do? You'd best look sharp and make your mind up while you still have a choice.' He moved over to the dresser and pulled out the wad of money that he'd been paid for the honey. 'You can take this, you've earned it this last six months. If you take that you could be well away by the time the police get here.'

At first I found it difficult to look at the pile of notes as it lay there on the table. I remembered the day that money had last lain there, what had gone before and what I had said to Susan then about running away, taking the money with us. I had always told myself I hadn't meant it. The thought of that heated my cheeks. I forced myself to pick the notes up. Moses watched me as if it was no concern of his. I turned the money over in my hand.

'Thanks, Moses, but I'll stay. I've stopped running.' I handed the money back to him. He smiled when I did that as if he was pleased at my choice. I didn't realise until later that my staying would cost him most.

There were no flashing lights and sirens when the police car pulled up outside the cottage. As Moses and I stood in the yard watching a constable coming towards us I suddenly, illogically, wondered if this was the police car who's flashing lights had made me leave the main road and come up the lane to find Moses nine months ago.

'Live out in the wilds don't you, Dad?' the policeman remarked as he drew level with us and I knew from that moment that neither Moses nor I were going to like him. 'I never knew anyone lived right out here. We've got it down as "void".'

'Void?' scowled Moses. 'What's void?'

'Empty, Dad. Derelict.'

'You'd better come inside,' Moses turned his back on us and led the way.

'Ta.' He removed his cap and set it on the table to remind us of his importance. His hair was red and curly, it looked garish in this sombre kitchen. His professional eye took in the room at a glance. He wrinkled his nose at the oil-lamp. 'Bit of a dump, this!'

'You don't have to like it,' Moses said indifferently. 'I do. Sit down, if you're stopping.'

The man sat down and reached into the breast pocket of his uniform for the inevitable notebook. There were splodgy freckles on the backs of his hands and thin ginger hairs sprouted from the thick white fingers.

'You're the young chap half the police of Britain have been

131

looking for?' he turned glinting green eyes on me that made me think of bounty-hunters in Westerns. He couldn't resist the relish of the capture even though he had nothing to do with that, that was Charlie's doing. 'How long have you been holed up here?'

'All the time. Nine months.'

'Let's get it all down. Name?'

Of course he knew my name perfectly well. If he hadn't why else was he there? But there was a form. I was getting my first touch of the civilised world again. I had been naughty and in the real world this was how naughty boys are treated.

He wanted facts, I gave him those, that was easy if only because it left everything of importance out and it was soon over.

'But you must have been out,' he said when I'd finished. 'Why didn't anyone see you?'

'I never walked down the lane past the farm. Moses posted the card to my mother. Apart from that I stayed here and just went for walks in the woods.'

'Yes,' said the policeman, looking at his notebook to stop himself winking at me but unable to keep the leer out of his voice, 'I've heard about your walks in the woods.'

I've never felt like hitting anybody before in my life but I swear that if I'd had Moses' axe handy I would have split the smug, red curls on that policeman's skull! He'd made me feel silly and cheap, maybe I was, but he made Susan sound cheap too and that idea I couldn't stand. I bit back my anger, I knew I wasn't in a position to call the shots.

'No wonder you wanted something to do, stuck up here.'

'There was always plenty to do. I helped Moses.'

'Moses. Yes, I didn't catch your other name?'

'I didn't give it. Beech.'

'Moses Beech,' he jotted that down in his little book, not that he was likely to forget it. 'You knew this lad was a runaway and that we were looking for him, why didn't you report him?' Moses stared stonily across the table. 'You not only concealed him but you persuaded Mr Bailey to do the same. I gather he

132

wishes he hadn't now. You could have saved us all a lot of bother if you'd turned this lad in straight away. I should imagine somebody will have something to say about that.' He paused to let his words sink in, then slowly rose to his feet. 'I'd better have a look round while I'm here. If you don't mind?'

'Can I stop you?' inquired Moses.

'You can if you like, but I'd like to see this young man's room.'

'Please yourself!'

I pushed open the door to my room and the policeman ducked his head and went in.

'These your belongings?' he nodded at the few clothes and things scattered about the room. He picked up the duffel bag and scattered its contents on the bed. He was clearly looking for stolen property but there was nothing that a blind man would have taken on a dark night. 'Nothing else?'

I shook my head. Looking around the room I had to agree that it was a poor showing for almost a year of living. He kicked the rough mattress with the glinting toe of his shoe.

'Is that straw in that?' he said showing his distaste. 'Not very comfortable.'

His look made the room seem so squalid. He only saw the rough, unmade bed and the mouldy paintwork. He couldn't know of the summer days I had lain on that mattress watching the clouds drift past in a pure, blue sky, nor of the times Susan and I had held each other there, those were things he couldn't nudge with the toe of his shoe.

'Where's the old man sleep?'

I showed him the small back room where I, and later Susan, had nursed the old man, probably the room he'd slept in all his life.

'What a smell! The whole house is riddled with damp. Hasn't he got any proper blankets?' he gingerly turned over the selection of clothing Moses kept piled on his bed for warmth. 'Poor old fellow.'

'He says he's got all he wants.'

We clumped down the uncarpeted stairs and stood awkwardly together in front of the range.

133

'You've let this place get in a bit of a state, Dad, if you don't mind my saying so.'

'You can say what you like, it suits me.'

'Well, we'll see,' he turned to me. 'We've tried to get in touch with your parents, but there was nobody at home.'

That didn't come as a surprise! Nobody realised I'd gone and now I was found nobody cared.

'We don't want to haul you off to jail, just yet,' he attempted a grin but neither of us was in the mood for jokes. 'So you'll have to stay here for the night until we can make arrangements.'

He picked his hat up off the table and walked over to the door.

'I'm holding you responsible for him, Dad,' he said with another silly grin, 'but, just in case you get any daft ideas, I'd like you to know I'm on duty tonight and I shall be up and down that main road fairly regular.'

His red hair and face went out through the door like our own personal sunset and we stood and welcomed back the silence that his presence had shattered.

'Typical copper!' I said at last.

'He's got a job to do; it wasn't likely we'd like him much, was it?'

I looked around the room unable to believe that soon I would be leaving for good. The reality of what had happened was slowly beginning to sink in.

'I'd better go and say goodbye to Susan. I don't expect there'll be time tomorrow.'

'You'd best stop here!' Moses said emphatically. 'If you go down there you'll come back with your head in a sling!'

'But I can't just go without saying a word,' I protested. Whatever Moses and I had gone through with the policeman would have been a child's tea-party compared to the unleashing of the holocaust that she'd experienced.

'You could write a letter,' Moses suggested without taking his eyes from the fire. I could tell his mind had gone back to the parting from Joseph.

There was nothing else for it, Moses was quite right. If I'd gone down to the farm Charlie would at best have set the dogs on me, and if I'd waited until I was whisked off to civilisation and phoned her they probably still wouldn't let me speak to her, and in the meantime she'd imagine I'd just left without a thought for her.

Moses turned the radio on and I settled down to compose my thoughts into some kind of order to a background of Moses sucking on his pipe and spitting in the fire, and Tchaikovsky.

I wanted to tell her I was sorry and that I regretted what had happened but that wasn't it at all. There was so much that I didn't regret and wouldn't have changed.

My eye wandered up from the blank unfriendly page to things which had become so much part of my life, the oil-lamp, the floral wallpaper that peeled away from the damp patches, and I tried to see it with the policeman's eyes, but I couldn't. All I saw was a kind of haven.

I looked at Moses, dozing over his pipe, and tried to feel for him the pity that the policeman obviously felt, but again I couldn't. All I saw was somebody who was his own person, who had taken me in when I needed help and who'd left me free to make my own decisions. He'd taught me a lot, probably more than I realised, about growing up and finding myself.

How he'd managed to cope with me when I came from a world so foreign to him, was more than I could understand. He'd managed to teach me practical things without shouting at me, as Dad always had. If it was going to be hard to leave Susan, it was going to be just as hard to leave Moses.

At the thought of Susan I picked up the pen and pushed it reluctantly across the page. It came out very trite in the end. I told her that I was sorry that things had turned out so badly, that I was sorry that there was so much she had to face alone, that I loved her and would try to see her again as soon as I could. It seemed pathetically inadequate.

'I've finished,' I said as I handed him the letter.

'That's good,' he said and tucked it into his bib pocket without a glance. Again the room fell silent but for the music and the clock.

I had found it hard to write to Susan but here was Moses

sitting in front of me and yet there was no way I could say any of
the things I wanted to tell him.

In the end, I said nothing.

Chapter 17

To avoid the awkward silences of the previous night we went out into the garden straight after breakfast and started to dig over the ground ready for the winter. I couldn't get it into my head that I wouldn't be there to see the results.

A mist hung over the entire valley, the leaves of the trees hung brown and damp. Our ears strained as we worked, for the sounds of the police car which would bring my parents. Several times we stopped work as we heard a car slow down on the main road only to hear it drive on through the muffled blanket of the mist.

As neither of us was getting any pleasure out of the work, we were just going through the motions to pass the time, we were almost relieved when at last a car did fight its way uncertainly up the lane and I prepared my mind and my stomach for what lay ahead.

We were both surprised when a woman walked round the corner of the building. Not a policewoman either, unless she was in plain clothes. She was tidily dressed and carried a black, plastic briefcase. There was no sign of my parents and it wasn't me she was interested in.

'Moses Beech?' She smiled and held out her hand which he seemed reluctant to shake. 'I'm Mrs Norbrook. I'd like to have a chat with you, if I may?'

Moses grunted a reply and then led the way into the kitchen.

'Would you like a cup of tea?' I made the offer largely as an excuse to stay and listen.

'If you're having one,' she replied. She had a kind face but it was reserved. Her glance round the room was quick and professional, like the policeman's the night before, but not as critical.

As I made the tea she took a black plastic folder from the briefcase, which she laid on the table, and, from her handbag, a yellow ball-point pen. I looked at it, feeling like a caveman. It looked so slick and garish, a harsh reminder of the world to which I was returning.

'I'm a Health Visitor with the County Council.'

'Yes,' Moses hissed sadly, 'I've been expecting you.'

'Oh, really?' she brightened visibly, missing the tone of Moses' voice. 'Well, if I'd known about you I'd have been here before. The policeman who came about Peter rang me this morning. He was worried about you and thought I ought to call.'

'He would.'

'Incidentally, Peter, the police are still having trouble contacting your parents. It seems it may be tomorrow before they can come and collect you.'

'Thanks,' I poured the tea and passed it round.

'Now, Mr Beech . . . .'

'Moses.'

'Pardon?'

'Moses. Everyone calls me Moses. The only person who ever called me Mr Beech wanted to tell me off, so I don't reckon it as a compliment.'

'All right, Moses.' She said it, but it made her uncomfortable, as if it made the conversation too personal.

'I suppose you're going to ask a lot of questions.'

'Just a few,' she admitted.

'I hope you're going to like the answers as much as you like asking the questions.'

'We'll have to see, won't we?' she smiled brightly. She started off with date and place of birth and the yellow pen twinkled merrily across the form. Then the pen hovered for a moment and

138

looked more like a dagger. 'The strange thing is Mr . . . Moses, I've been going through the records and I can't find your National Insurance number.'

'Biscuit?' I said sweetly. 'Moses is renowned for his ginger biscuits.'

'No. Thank you.' She didn't take her eyes off Moses for a second.

'Is that right?' he reached out, took a biscuit and dunked it in his tea.

'Would you happen to know it? – It would help, for the form.'

'I wouldn't,' he sucked the biscuit noisily.

'What about your medical card?'

'I haven't got one.'

'No medical card?' she laid the pen down on the form.

'I haven't seen a doctor since I was a lad. My Mam took me with a septic finger and we paid cash on the nail.'

Mrs Norbrook couldn't believe her ears. Nor could I. I should have realised when he said he didn't get the pension, but I hadn't. I hugged myself with glee, I was beginning to enjoy this.

'But what about your Insurance contributions when you worked?'

'Never paid none.'

'None at all?'

'You've got my date of birth. I've never paid nothing, nor got nothing. And what's more, I don't want nothing.'

'But what about your pension? You're probably entitled to Social Security payments, rent and rate rebates, all that sort of thing.'

'I don't get no pension. I don't want to go on the Poor. I've seen them, worked hard all their lives and then taken off to the workhouse. They only asked for a bit of help, but next thing they know they're in the workhouse.'

'That was years ago, that sort of thing doesn't happen these days.'

'Oh, no?' he fixed her with his eye, 'then what are you asking all these questions for? Writing me down on your form?'

'I only want to help,' she said earnestly. She picked up the pen but it hung like a halted pendulum from her fingers. Against Moses it appeared redundant, helpless. He didn't fit the form.

'I don't need any help,' he said bluntly, then added as an afterthought, 'thank you, very much.'

'But it must be a struggle making ends meet. What about your rent and rates?'

'I don't suppose struggling has done me much harm. If it's any of your business, this cottage is mine. I've got a deed in a box under my bed for it. I've never had no call to pay rates.'

'No call?' The pen slipped from her fingers and rolled away unheeded. In her orderly world this was almost a sin.

'What do people pay rates for?'

'Education, Social Services, drainage, roads, even emptying your toilet. I presume you have an Elsan?'

'I have an earth closet, I empty it myself. As for the rest I don't use them. Except for the roads and I always was told it was the King's Highway.'

'I simply can't believe it. You don't exist. I mean, on paper.

'I'm in the Parish Register, if you care to look. Go to Church do you?'

'No . . . er . . . not often.'

'Neither do I. Funny really, with a name like Moses.'

'But Mr Beech, you can't have gone through the whole of your life without filling in a form. People would be bound to ask questions.'

'I couldn't fill in a form even if I wanted to, ask Peter.'

'It's quite true,' I nodded, 'Moses can't read or write, can you?'

'No,' he said and beamed at the poor, baffled lady.

'What about war service?'

'Agricultural worker? Everyone said I didn't have to go, so there didn't seem much point in filling in a form for that. They said I'd have to fill in forms for feed for pigs and poultry, but I managed. I even got sugar to feed the bees from Fred at the shop. We've known each other since we were kids, he didn't want no form.'

'What about your rations? You must have had ration books?'

140

'Why? I fed myself apart from tea and flour and there were plenty of people willing to swop me those for a bit of extra bacon or eggs.'

'I can't believe it,' she sat back in her chair utterly defeated by Moses who had attacked the very roots of the system which employed her.

'Put it this way, Miss, I didn't want anything, so why waste people's time filling up forms. Waste of time!'

'Well, I just don't know what to do!'

'You just go back to wherever it is you came from and leave me be.'

'It isn't that simple. You've been assigned to my case-load, a report will have to be made out. Now that we know you exist, we must assess your needs and see to them.'

'I know my needs and I look after them. I'm perfectly happy as I am.'

'We can't leave you like this, Mr Beech,' her words took in Moses, the room and the world at large. 'It simply wouldn't do. We live in a caring society.'

'You live in a nosy society! I live here and I'm quite content.'

'The house is in poor condition, you could be very ill if you stayed here for another winter.'

'I've been ill and I'm well again. Peter and the Baileys helped me.'

'Peter won't be here to help next time something goes wrong and the Baileys are too far away to help in an emergency.'

I remembered Moses' collapse in the bean row and had to admit to myself that it was lucky that Susan and I had been there to help. Heaven knows how long he would have lain there if we hadn't been handy.

'If I may, I'd like to look round while I'm here?' she got up from her chair with an air of determination and her black plastic file.

'He'll show you,' Moses said and poured himself another cup of tea.

While we walked round upstairs we didn't exchange a word. She looked at all three rooms and the yellow pen darted and

141

flashed across the paper. It was happier now that it was dealing with familiar things, tangible things that fitted its usual pattern, like damp or dirt.

When we went downstairs I took her into the parlour and she even insisted on visiting the dreaded earth-closet!

'Would you like to use it while you're here?' I offered in a burst of generosity.

'Not just now,' she said flatly and I closed the door on the newspaper hanging from its hook.

'Well, Mr Beech,' she began, all thoughts of Christian names had disappeared by now, 'I am going back to the office. There are some things to be sorted out.'

'Just as you like,' he said affably.

'In the mean time I'm going to ask a doctor to call and examine you.'

'I'm not paying. I'm perfectly all right.'

'There's nothing to pay. I just want you to have a check-up, it's a matter of routine.'

The black plastic file slipped into the briefcase and the yellow pen was restored to its lair.

'Nice of you to call,' Moses said as he heaved himself out of the chair and opened the door for her to leave.

'Oh, I shall be back as soon as the doctor's been. Goodbye for the time being,' she smiled and left us looking at each other.

'I'm sorry, Moses,' I said, picking at the newspaper on the table with a restless finger. 'I've brought all this on you, haven't I?'

'It would have happened sooner or later anyway.'

'I didn't realise you were in hiding too, no wonder you didn't want the police coming up here.'

'I've not been in hiding from anybody, I just wanted to be left alone. I didn't want busybodies poking their noses in. Oh, I'm sure they mean well, and there's lots of people, worse off than me, who'd be glad of their help, but I just wanted to be left in peace.'

'I'm sorry I got you into this.'

'Don't bother your head about it. If it wasn't you it would

have been somebody else. Charlie Bailey's threatened to get them up here many a time but I always managed to put him off. I'll manage just one more year, I used to say. Well, it looks as if time's run out.'

The doctor, a small man with a wispy moustache, arrived in the early afternoon and spent half an hour poking and prodding poor old Moses. I'd expected the old man to object strongly and refuse to let the doctor touch him as loudly as he'd shouted at us when we'd suggested getting help before, but he didn't, he just accepted his fate like a lamb.

An hour or so after the doctor left Mrs Norbrook was back. I doubt if the house had had so many visitors in one day for years.

My offers of tea were instantly rejected. The briefcase stayed in the car, even the yellow pen didn't appear.

'Mr Beech, I want you to go into Deanside. It's one of our smaller houses and I'm sure you'd be very comfortable. The doctor says you need some medical attention and it would be better if you were at Deanside for that,' she paused to let the news sink in. 'Now, I don't want you to think of this as a permanent arrangement. It's only temporary, and of course you'll be able to leave if ever you want to.'

Moses scuffed at the rug with the toe of his boot but he didn't say anything.

'It's for your own good, Mr Beech,' she said earnestly and you could see she honestly meant it. 'The doctor says you've had heart trouble, you could have another attack at any time.'

'The Baileys always watch for me smoke. They'd come.'

'But if it happened at night nobody would find you until the next day, and that might be too late. Your lungs are not good either. Mr Beech you've worked hard all your life, I can see that, and I admire your independence, but it's time to let others do their bit.'

'I could stay and look after him,' I blurted out.

'No, Peter. Thanks all the same for the offer, I appreciate it, but you've got your own life to lead.'

'Perhaps Mum and Dad would let you come and live with us,' I was getting desperate to rescue Moses.

'Where do you live, Peter?' Mrs Norbrook asked quietly.

'Two bedroom flat in a high-rise block,' I knew what she was getting at.

'And I gather your father isn't entirely able to support the family as it is?' she pointed out reasonably. 'There is no other solution, I'm afraid. Deanside is a very nice place; many people would be glad of the chance to go there.'

'Let them go then!'

'We feel your case is more urgent. You'll soon make friends. They have a nice sun lounge and television.'

Moses snorted.

'I know how upsetting it is to leave somewhere you've lived all your life, but your health is at risk. If you go to Deanside you'll probably live for years.'

'To do what? Sit in the sun lounge,' Moses said with utter contempt. 'Do I have any choice?'

'As the doctor says that you would be at serious risk if you remain in this house, whether alone or with help, then there are means of protecting you from yourself.'

'In other words, you could force me?'

'I wouldn't put it like that.'

'It comes to the same thing,' Moses glowered at the ground in front of him. 'Do you want me to pack now?'

'Good heavens no! There are arrangements to be made. Pack a few things and I'll call for you tomorrow morning at ten.'

Moses nodded and she got up to go. This time he made no effort to show her out but she paused in the doorway.

'If you really don't like it at Deanside, you can come back, I promise,' she said. Moses let out a silent, scoffing laugh and she left.

'I always thought,' he said softly, 'that if I didn't ask for anything, didn't have a number, they'd leave me alone to do things my own way. I told her I never paid nothing, that I didn't have a number, but it doesn't seem to matter.'

'Don't go. She can't make you.'

'Once they get their hooks into you they can always find ways of making you do what they want.'

144

It was really ironic! Moses was being forced to accept what my Dad had been trying to get all his life, a free ride.

'They get you in the end,' he said and let out a deep sigh of regret.

Chapter 18

'*I*'D like some time to myself tonight,' Moses announced when the supper things were put away. 'I've got things to sort out, I'd like to leave things straight.'

'That's all right. I'll go for a walk in the wood. It doesn't matter who sees me now!'

There was hardly any moon, the mist was still hanging over the valley like a cloak. Columns of rose-bay willow-herb lined the path, in the half light, like ageing sentries. The remaining pink flowers drooped over the white whiskery seeds. Heavy with the damp they were unable to blow away and colonise new ground.

I paused at the lichen encrusted, weather-worn, wicket gate. The mist hung around the tops of the pine trees and the wood seemed dank and unfriendly tonight. I shivered slightly and passed on through the gate. As I did I thought I heard a footstep behind me but when I stopped I could hear nothing.

It was too dark to use the narrow side-paths so I stuck to the wide main ride that cuts its way through the centre of the wood. No owls hunted that night.

A stick snapped somewhere in the wood and I felt eyes on the back of my neck although when I turned round there was nobody to see. I stepped off the track behind the coarse trunk of a pine tree and waited. I was certain now that I was not alone in the wood. Perhaps the policeman had been keeping an eye on the cottage in case I should try to run away again. I decided to give him a run for his money if that was true.

I waited for what seemed like hours before I heard a stone rasping in protest under the weight of somebody's shoe. I contained my curiosity. If I peered out, they would certainly see me but if I stayed still, flattened against the tree trunk they probably wouldn't notice me and when they had passed I could slip out and set off in the opposite direction.

The footsteps were very near now and my eyes strained through the dusk in preparation to catch every detail. It was a figure huddled in a dark donkey jacket, with wellington boots and some sort of cap pulled well down. I hardly dared to turn my head as they passed but at the last second I caught a glimpse of blonde hair and as a twig snapped under my feet the head swung round and I saw the glint of glasses!

'Susan!'

'Oh, you made me jump,' she recovered her breath and fell into my arms. I kissed her neck, burying my nose in the sharp crisp smell of her hair.

'What were you doing creeping about?' I asked.

'I had to be sure it was you. I'd just come out for a walk. I wanted to come and see you both to see what had happened but I knew it would only make things worse if Dad found out, so I came up here instead. Then I saw somebody ahead of me on the track but I couldn't tell if it was you or a poacher. I thought I'd better make sure before I rushed up to them and threw my arms round their neck.'

For a moment we stood in silence gazing at each other, each searching the other's face, then I turned and started to walk up the track and Susan fell into step beside me.

'What has happened?' she asked quietly.

'The police came and my parents are coming to get me. The welfare people came and the doctor. They want Moses to go into a home.'

'I was afraid they would.'

'It's all my stupid fault. The whole mess,' I said bitterly.

'Mine too, Peter,' she spoke so quietly in the stillness of the wood as if the trees might hear.

'But if I hadn't run away none of this would ever have

147

happened. Moses would be able to live in peace, instead of which they're carting him off tomorrow.'

'If you hadn't arrived, Peter, Moses would probably be dead. You nursed him through that first attack during the snow.'

'All right, but you wouldn't be pregnant.'

'I'm not,' she said softly. She had stopped abruptly in the middle of the track.

'What?' I walked back to her.

'It was a false alarm. My period started this morning.'

For a moment I couldn't speak, I just bit my lower lip and tried to sort out my thoughts.

'So there was no need to call the police? Moses would never have got a visit from the welfare people. Damn! Damn everything!' I savagely kicked at a stone.

'It can't be helped, it's just one of those things,' she rested her hand on my arm.

'The stupid part is,' I said, calming down a bit, 'I'm almost sorry that you're not pregnant. I meant what I said about getting married. I'd still like to, one day.'

'No, Peter,' she was almost whispering now. Her face looked pinched as if she were resisting pain.

'Why not?' I couldn't understand her talking like this. She couldn't have forgotten what we meant to each other so soon?

'Because after what's happened nothing will ever be quite the same again. Dad will never forgive you. We betrayed a trust. Eventually he'll forgive me, but not you. Like lots of big, tough men he doesn't really show his feelings much, except when he's angry, but they go very deep.'

'You can't let him spoil our happiness.'

'It would anyway, don't you see? It's not as if we could get married for years and all the time they'd be watching, perhaps begrudging.'

'But I love you, Susan,' I was shaking her to make her understand.

'I love you too. I'll never forget you. I'll always be glad we met. It's just that things haven't worked out as they should have, or perhaps they have, I don't know.'

148

We turned and started to walk slowly back towards the gate. I felt utterly flattened and defeated.

'Dad's given in over my Commercial Design Course.'

'That's good.'

'He said I can take the course. It cost him a lot to agree to that. I think he was trying to soften the hurt for me. What are you going to do now?'

'Whatever they say, what else?'

'Oh, Peter! All this for nothing? You can't just go back and give in, you can't!'

'What else am I supposed to do? I've got everything wrong. I thought I knew so much!'

The mist had turned to rain now. It speckled our clothes and splashed her glasses, causing them to mist over.

'Damn these things,' she snatched them off, stuffed them in the pocket of her donkey jacket and grabbed my hand to lead her back to the gate.

After we'd passed through the gate we stopped. I took her ridiculous cap off and tucked that in her pocket then I cupped her face in my hands so that I could feel the cool hair flowing over my fingers. Droplets of rain trickled down her upturned face. Neither of us knew how to end the conversation and the silence hung heavily between us. If one of us didn't break it soon it would become impossible.

'I hope everything sorts itself out,' I said lamely.

'It will.'

'I hope you get over me, all this, soon.'

'I don't suppose I'll ever really "get over" it, but I expect I'll learn to live with it, one day.' She reached up kissed me on the cheek, then pulling her glasses out she pushed them on as she ran away, stumbling down the hill. I think she was crying. I know I was.

I followed her slowly down the track. Long after she was out of earshot I heard the farm dogs barking and I knew she was home.

I walked through the damp yard to the cottage door. It was no longer my home, I was going *there* tomorrow! I suddenly realised the door was wide open but there were no lights on. There was no sound or movement inside and the fire had burnt low in the grate. I was suddenly afraid that the strain of the last couple of days might have produced one final heart attack and that while I was up in the wood Moses had died alone.

'Moses,' I shouted. My voice echoed around the kitchen.

'It's all right, lad. I was just sitting here thinking.'

'I got frightened when I didn't see any lights,' I struck a match and lit the oil lamp. It stood alone in the centre of the table. While I'd been away Moses had certainly been tidying up! Gone was the clutter, gone too the newspapers. The lamp alone stood on the plain, white, scrubbed surface of the table which reflected back the light like a tombstone awaiting an inscription.

'I saw Susan up by the wood. She isn't going to have a baby.' He nodded but said nothing. 'We said goodbye, so there's no need to give her the letter.'

He fished around the bib pocket and gave me back the envelope which was folded in two. I stuffed it into my pocket without looking at it.

We both had too much to think about to talk and we were anxious to get to our rooms. Even carrying the candle up the stairs made me think of my return to the world of electricity the following day.

I lay awake for hours that night on the mattress the policeman had despised, the mattress that had supported my aching back after each hard day's work, the mattress Susan and I had shared. My mattress.

As I lay there thinking of the future and remembering the past, I heard a noise coming from Moses' room. At first I thought he must be dreaming, making noises in his sleep, but I realised he was crying. Crying alone in his room, there was nothing I could do to help.

Chapter 19

I WOKE up to find the sun streaming in through the window. I had fallen asleep in the early hours of the morning and now the day was bright and cloudless as if to mock us.

Moses had done such an efficient job on cleaning up it seemed a shame to disturb things and neither of us felt like eating anyway. After a cup of coffee I went with Moses to feed the pig and the chickens.

'I'll stop off at the farm,' he said, 'and ask Charlie to look after them.'

As we walked back to the house Moses found a trowel we'd left out. He insisted on taking it to the shed with the rest of the tools although for the life of me I couldn't see that it mattered any more even if it rusted away in the garden.

I came back from the dreaded lavatory, one aspect of living with Moses I'd be only too glad to leave, to find him emptying the sink-bucket on to the garden. Then he emptied the last of the water from the kettle on the fire. A cloud of steam hissed up the chimney until the last of the heat was gone and the ashes lay dull and grey.

As the clock struck ten we heard a car coming up the lane. Together we went over to the window to look. In fact there were two cars. A big red and white police car led the way and Mrs Norbrook's Mini followed.

Moses went and sat in his armchair. He never liked much fuss and I thought he wanted me to meet my parents outside so that the excitement would be over before they came into the house.

I left my duffel bag leaning against his old canvas holdall just inside the door and stepped out into the sunshine, uncertain what to expect. Reunions in films always show cries of delight as the people run towards each other. I couldn't see that happening with us. Too much had happened to hold us apart instead of draw us close.

My mother and father were in the back of the car. I'd always expected to see my Dad sitting in a police car one day, but not quite like this. Mum got out first, looking around to take in the surroundings, she stumbled. Her heels were smart for the city streets but impractical in the country lane.

'We've come for our son,' she said proudly to me, as if she was talking to the manager of a Bingo Hall where she'd just won the Snowball. She didn't recognise me!

'I am your son,' I said flatly.

'Well, you do look a sight!'

My hair hadn't been cut since I'd arrived. My jeans, though clean, were torn, patched and fraying. My jersey barely reached my wrists, I'd filled out a good deal from the hard physical work I'd been doing, and my skin was the same rich brown as Moses'. To her I must have looked like Robinson Crusoe.

'More like a tramp,' Dad said as he came up beside her.

'Now, Dad! He's safe and well, that's the main thing.'

'I suppose you realise your mother's been worried out of her mind?' he said sharply.

'Dad! We'll talk about that later,' she said and he subsided while she gave me a hug.

'Is Mr Beech ready?' Mrs Norbrook broke in.

'I think so,' I said as I turned and led the party towards the yard.

'Yes, I've got a few things I'd like to say to him,' Dad mumbled darkly. 'For a start, I want to know . . . .'

A sharp explosion cut his sentence short. A startled arc of black lapwings curved up from the field and flashed its white, protesting belly at us as we stood frozen, clinging to the last echo of the sound which had split the morning. As the birds wheeled off in regained formation I broke away from our group and raced towards the house.

'Moses! Moses!' The words were torn from my throat but I knew they were useless.

He lay huddled outside the kitchen door. His dark blood traced the map of his departure on the cold, blue brick of the yard. The old shot-gun, casually smoking like a cigarette lodged temporarily in an ashtray, lay across his dead body. I threw it away, fell to my knees and hugged his still warm body as my tears skidded off the grease of his jacket.

Shadows fell across me as I rocked him backwards and forwards repeating his name over and over again. Hands pulled me away and I was being bundled into the police car. Somebody said, stupidly, as if it might change something 'He shot himself.'

'No,' I shouted, 'I killed him!'

For days I wandered round the flat. Nothing felt right. I'd got used to wood with grain, weight and texture; here there was only lifeless plastic. I remembered the feel of bricks, soil and grass; now there was only concrete as far as the eye could see. The china ducks were no substitute for the real thing. Even the simplest things like light switches and taps seemed not only to defeat me but also to serve as reminders of the past. Sitting at home surrounded by wall to wall boredom with not even the prospect of the next round of the Great Mousing Contest to look forward to, it was a long time before I really began to take things in and realise there had been some changes while I'd been away.

For a start they didn't row much any more. There was still some nit picking but no all out shouting matches. Mum only went to Bingo once a week and, most surprising of all, Dad had got a job!

I really didn't expect that to last. Every day when he came home I expected him to say he'd either been sacked or he'd jacked it in, but he never did. He also kept asking me questions about living with Moses. Mum would try to shut him up because I think she thought it brought everything back again, but I was

153

glad of the chance to talk about it. After all it had been a way of life for nearly a year and I was missing it like hell.

At first I'd expected him to pour scorn on everything I told him about the gardening, the cooking and everything, but he didn't. In fact he looked quite wistful sometimes and I began to get an idea he was almost jealous of the life I'd had, in some ways. Maybe living in this concrete jungle had made him into the man I knew.

So we never had the row Dad had promised: they did special things for me, Mum cooked my favourite food but I still woke up in cold sweats screaming from nightmares centred on the last day with Moses. Mum would come in and hug me quiet and I felt like a little kid again.

It went on for a couple of months like that and the doctor kept coming and prescribing pills but I knew pills couldn't cure me. I found out that Mum had been on tranquillizers while I'd been away but she didn't need them now. In some strange way I seemed to have solved some of their problems and none of my own.

'What are you going to do, Peter?' Dad asked one night. 'You can't stay moping around here for ever.'

'Leave him alone,' Mum leapt in, all protective. She looked younger these days and her eyes seemed brighter than I had remembered. 'There's time enough for that.'

'No, Mum, Dad's right. It's time I tried to do something, otherwise living like this could become a habit,' I swallowed hard before the last bit. 'I want to go back to school.'

I waited for the walls to fall in, for all the goodwill that had built up to evaporate, but it didn't.'

'After all this time?' Mum was the one to break the silence.

'It's the only way. I never really wanted to leave school, that's really what all this has been about. If I go back, get some more exams, then I might know what I really want to do. After all, I've only got one chance and I'd like to try it my way.' The room was very quiet. 'I feel I owe at least that to Moses as well.'

In the end it hasn't quite worked out like that. I did go back to school but it was useless, I couldn't just slip back into my old life that easily. Going back to books and learning was hard enough but all the kids had read about me, seen me on the telly, and they would never let me forget it for a moment.

Eventually I left again and I've got a job in a shop.

In a way Dad got his way, but I'm also going to evening classes and I'm determined that I'll get my way too. I never got in touch with Susan. If things work out, maybe I will, one day, but if I do I want to have something to tell her.

Yesterday Mum was clearing out junk from my room. Time and again she's wanted to throw away my old jeans and shirt that I wore that last day, but I wouldn't let her, even though they were spattered with Moses' blood. I always felt they were the last tangible link and when they were gone there would be nothing.

But perhaps it shows I'm getting stronger now. I said she could get rid of them. Out of habit she checked the pockets and pulled out the letter I'd written to Susan, all crumpled and forgotten.

'I'll have that,' I said. I was just going to tear it up when I realised there was something else folded inside. It was the deed to Moses' house.

The fine, frail paper, as dry as skin, is lying in front of me now. The spidery copperplate writing hypnotises me. I remember the words that went with that deed as it first passed into the hands of the Beech family.

'In recognition of devotion above the average,' Moses had said. I know I haven't earned it yet but I'm trying.

One day I might go back to that house – if I can stand the pain.